The Eternal Wisdom

The Eternal Wisdom

**Central Sayings of Great Sages
of All Times**

SRI AUROBINDO ASHRAM
PONDICHERRY, INDIA

First serialised in the monthly review *Arya* 1914-21
First edition (part only) 1922
First complete edition of *Arya* sayings 1993
Second impression 1995

(Typeset in 11/14 point Palatino)

PB. ISBN 81-7058-319-5
HB. ISBN 81-7058-320-9

Published by Sri Aurobindo Ashram Publication Department
Printed at Sri Aurobindo Ashram Press, Pondicherry
PRINTED IN INDIA

Publisher's Note

The Eternal Wisdom is a collection of the sayings of great thinkers and sages of the East and West. Representing a wide spectrum of spiritual and philosophic traditions, it spans a period of five thousand years, from the time of the Rig-veda to the present. The collection was first published between 1914 and 1921 in monthly instalments of *Arya*, a philosophical review edited by Sri Aurobindo. It was Sri Aurobindo who translated the sayings from French into English, with the exception of biblical quotations, which follow, with very minor differences, the King James version of the Bible. When *Arya* ceased in January 1921, only two-thirds of the compilation had appeared; the final third was never issued. The first half of the sayings in *Arya* were brought out in 1992 in a book of the same title published by Ganesh & Co., Madras. The present book contains the entire collection of published sayings.

Contents

CONTENTS

BOOK TWO

The Discovery and Conquest of the Divine in Oneself

Section I

The Conquest of Truth

Section II

The Practice of Truth

Section III

The Conquest of Self

CONTENTS

Section IV

The Victory of the Divine

BOOK THREE

The Union of All in the One in All

Section I

Death and Immortality

Section II

The Unity of All

Section III

The Practice of Love

CONTENTS

Section IV

The Solidarity of All

INTRODUCTION

The Song of Wisdom

We fight to win sublime Wisdom; therefore men call us warriors.

Book of Wisdom

Put Wisdom at the head of the world; the world will fight its battle victoriously and will be the best world that men can constitute.

Carlyle

This Wisdom is the principle of all things.

Zohar

This mysterious Wisdom is the supreme principle of all.

Zohar

**

I. Wisdom, dwell with prudence and find out knowledge of witty inventions.... Counsel is mine and sound knowledge. I am understanding. I am strength. By me Kings reign and princes decree justice. By me princes rule, and nobles, even all the judges of the earth. I love them that love me. And those that seek me shall find me. Riches and honour are with me; yea, durable riches and righteousness. My fruit is better than gold, yea, than fine gold; and my revenue than choice silver. I lead in the way of righteousness, in the midst of the paths of judgment, that I may cause those that love me to inherit substance; and I will fill their treasures.... I was set up from everlasting, from the beginning before ever the earth was. When there were no depths, I was brought forth; when there were no fountains abounding with water, before the mountains were settled, before the hills were, I was brought forth.

Proverbs

I am the mother of pure love and of science and of sacred hope.

Ecclesiasticus

Wisdom is a thing of which one can never have enough.

Minokhired

Wisdom is the most precious riches.

Chinese Buddhist Scripture

How much better is it to get wisdom than gold! and to get understanding rather to be chosen than silver!

Proverbs

To have wisdom is worth more than pearls.

Job

Happy is the man that findeth wisdom and the man that getteth understanding. For the merchandise of it is better than the merchandise of silver and the gain thereof than fine gold. She is more precious than rubies and all the things thou canst desire are not to be compared unto her. Her ways are ways of pleasantness, and all her paths

are peace. She is a tree of life to them that lay hold
on her, and happy is everyone that retaineth her.

Proverbs

The possession of wisdom leadeth to true
happiness.

Porphyry

In this state of pure felicity the soul is en-
larged and the material substance that is subject to
her profiteth also.

Tseng Tse

Wisdom strengtheneth the wise more than
ten mighty men which are in a city.

Ecclesiasticus

Wisdom is greater than all terrestrial sciences and than all human knowledge. She renders
a man indifferent to the joys of the world and
permits him to consider with an impassive heart
their precipitous and tumultuous course.

Fa-ken-pi-u

A happy life is the fruit of wisdom achieved; life bearable, of wisdom commenced.

Seneca

Wisdom is a well-spring of life unto him that hath it.

Proverbs

Who loves her loves life and they that keep vigil to find her shall enjoy her peace. Whosoever possesses her, shall have life for his inheritance.

Ecclesiasticus

Of all our possessions, wisdom alone is immortal.

Socrates

The desire for wisdom leads us to the Eternal Kingdom.

Book of Wisdom

Wisdom is full of light and her beauty is not withered.

Book of Wisdom

Wisdom is like unto a beacon set on high, which radiates its light even in the darkest night.

Japanese Buddhist Meditations

And when the benevolence of benevolences manifests itself, all things are in her light and in joy.

Zohar

That which satisfies the soul is the wisdom which governs the world.

Lalita Vistara

Honour to the high and sublime excellence of wisdom!

Mahayana Buddhist Formula of Devotion

But where shall wisdom be found? and where is the place of understanding?

Job

As the light of a torch illumines the objects in a dark room, even so the light of wisdom illumines all men, whosoever they be, if they turn towards it.

Fo-shu-hing-tsan-king

Those who love her discover her easily and those that seek her do find her.

Book of Wisdom

Wisdom is a thing vast and grand. She demands all the time that one can consecrate to her.

Seneca

To find our real being and know it truly is to acquire wisdom.

Porphyry

Only by falling back on our better thought, by yielding to the spirit of prophecy which is innate in every man, can we know what that wisdom saith.

Emerson

The beginning of wisdom is the sincere desire for instruction. To observe attentively its laws is to establish the perfect purity of the soul.

Book of Wisdom

Behold the beginning of wisdom; therefore get wisdom; and with all thy getting, get understanding. Exalt her and she shall promote thee. She shall bring thee to honour, when thou dost embrace her. She shall give to thine head an ornament of grace; a crown of glory shall she deliver to thee.

Proverbs

Thou shalt invest thyself with her as with a raiment of glory and thou shalt put her on thy head as a crown of joy.

Ecclesiasticus

Say unto wisdom, "Thou art my sister," and call understanding thy kinswoman.

Proverbs

For wisdom shall enter into thine heart and knowledge be pleasant unto thy soul.

Proverbs

*
**

Having thought of these things, meditating on them in my heart and having considered that I shall find immortality in the union with wisdom, I went in search of her on all sides, that I might take her for my companion.

Book of Wisdom

I have preferred wisdom to kingdoms and thrones and I have believed that riches are nothing before wisdom, for she is an endless treasure for men.

Book of Wisdom

I looked on all the works that my hands had wrought and on the labour that I had laboured to do; and behold, all was vanity and pursuit of the wind and there was no profit under the sun. And I turned myself to behold wisdom, and madness and folly.... Then I saw that wisdom excelleth folly, as far as light excelleth darkness.

Ecclesiasticus

I have learnt all that was hidden and all that was yet undiscovered because I was taught by wisdom herself that created everything. For there is in her a spirit of intelligence which is holy, unique, multiple in her effects, fine, copious, agile, spotless, dear, soft, friendly to good, penetrant, which nothing can prevent from acting, benevolent, friendly to men, kind, stable, infallible, calm, that achieves all, that sees all, that can comprehend all minds in itself, that is intelligible, pure and subtle.

Book of Wisdom

Eternal wisdom builds: I shall be her palace when she finds repose in me and I in her.

Angelus Silesius

Wisdom and the Religions

All wisdom is one: to understand the spirit that rules all by all.

Heraclitus

Being but one, she is capable of all; immutable in herself, she renews all things; she diffuses herself among the nations in saintly souls.

Book of Wisdom

The dayspring from on high has visited us, to give light to them that sit in the darkness and in the shadow of death, to guide our feet in the way of peace.

Luke

Whatsoever things were written aforetime, were written for our learning.

Romans

True knowledge does not grow old, so have declared the sages of all times.

Pali Canon

May the partisans of all doctrines in all countries unite and live in a common fellowship. For all alike profess mastery to be attained over oneself and purity of the heart.

Inscriptions of Ashoka

There is only one Ethics, as there is only one geometry. But the majority of men, it will be said, are ignorant of geometry. Yes, but as soon as they begin to apply themselves a little to that science, all are in agreement. Cultivators, workmen, artisans have not gone through courses in ethics; they have not read Cicero or Aristotle, but the moment they begin to think on the subject they become, without knowing it, the disciples of Cicero. The Indian dyer, the Tartar shepherd and the English sailor know what is just and what is unjust. Confucius did not invent a system of ethics as one invents a system of physics. He had discovered it in the heart of all mankind.

Voltaire

The sage's rule of moral conduct has its principle in the hearts of all men.

Tseng Tse

There is a primary law, eternal, invariable, engraved in the hearts of all; it is Right Reason. Never does it speak in vain to the virtuous man, whether it ordains or prohibits. The wicked alone are untouched by its voice. It is easy to be understood and is not different in one country and in another; it is today what it will be tomorrow and for all time.

Cicero

Language is different but man is the same everywhere. That is why spoken Reason is one, and through its translation we see it to be the same in Egypt, in Persia and in Greece.

Hermes

But in what circumstances does our reason teach us that there is vice or virtue? How does this continual mystery work? Tell me, inhabitants of the Malay Archipelago, Africans, Canadians and you, Plato, Cicero, Epictetus! You all feel equally that it is better to give away the superfluity of your bread, your rice or your manioc to the indigent than to kill him or tear out his eyes. It is evident to all on earth that an act of benevolence is better than an outrage, that gentleness is preferable to wrath. We have merely to use our Reason in order to discern the shades which distinguish right and wrong. Good and evil are often close neighbours and our passions confuse them. Who will enlighten us? We ourselves when we are calm.

Voltaire

*
**

In order to live a happy life, man should understand what life is and what he can or cannot do. The best and wisest men in all nations have taught it to us from all times. All the doctrines of the sages meet in their foundation and it is this general sum of their doctrines, revealing the aim of human life and the conduct to be pursued, that constitutes real religion.

Tolstoy

The man who does not think about religion, imagines that there is only one that is true, the one in which he was born. But thou hast only to ask thyself what would happen if thou wert born in another religion, thou, Christian, if thou wert born a Muhammadan, thou, Buddhist, a Christian, and thou, Muhammadan, a Brahmin. Is it possible that we alone with our religion should be in the truth and that all others should be subjected to falsehood? No religion can become true merely by thy persuading thyself or persuading others that it alone is true.

Tolstoy

No man has a right to constrain another to think like himself. Each must bear with patience and indulgence the beliefs of others.

Giordano Bruno

To compel men to do what appears good to oneself is the best means of making them disgusted with it.

Tolstoy

As one can go up to the top of a house by means of a ladder, a bamboo or a flight of stairs, so

are there various means for approaching the
Eternal and each religion in the world shows only
one of such means.

Ramakrishna

A truly religious man ought to think that the
other religions are also paths leading towards the
Reality. We should always maintain an attitude of
respect towards other religions.

Ramakrishna

Decry not other sects nor depreciate them
but, on the contrary, render honour to that in them
which is worthy of honour.

Inscriptions of Ashoka

The Catholic is our brother but the materialist
not less. We owe him deference as to the greatest
of believers.

Antoine the Healer

At a certain stage in the path of devotion the
religious man finds satisfaction in the Divinity

with a form, at another stage in the formless Impersonal.

Ramakrishna

The man who proclaims the existence of the Infinite accumulates, in this affirmation, more of the supernatural than there is in the miracles of all the religions. So long as the mystery of the Infinite weighs upon human thought, temples will be raised for the cult of the Infinite.

Pasteur

Bow down and adore where others bend the knee; for where so great a number of men pay the tribute of their adoration, the Impersonal must needs manifest Himself, for He is all compassion.

Ramakrishna

The ordinary man says in his ignorance, "My religion is the sole religion, my religion is the best." But when his heart is illumined by the true knowledge, he knows that beyond all the battles of sects and of sectaries presides the one, indivisible, eternal and omniscient Benediction.

Ramakrishna

BOOK ONE

THE GOD OF ALL
THE GOD WHO IS IN ALL

The Sole Essence

The Universe is a unity.

Philolaus

All is in the One in power and the One is in all in act.

Abraham ibn Ezra

The Essence of all things is one and identical.

Ashwaghosha

I looked on high and I beheld in all the spaces That which is One; below, in all the foam of the waters that which is One; I looked into the heart, it was a sea, a space for worlds peopled with thousands of dreams: I saw in all the dreams That which is One.

Jalal-uddin Rumi

All that exists is but the transformation of one and the same Matter and is therefore one and the same thing.

Diogenes of Apollonia

All souls are merely determinations of the universal Soul. Bodies taken separately are only varied and transient forms of material substance.

Kapila

The infinite variety of particular objects constitutes one sole and identical Being. To know that unity is the aim of all philosophy and of all knowledge of Nature.

Giordano Bruno

True knowledge leads to unity, ignorance to diversity.

Ramakrishna

The rays of the divine sun, the infinite Orient, shine equally on all that exists and the illumination of Unity repeats itself everywhere.

Baha-ullah

The Universe is a unity.

Anaxagoras

In the world of the Unity heaven and earth are one.

Baha-ullah

We share one Intelligence with heaven and the stars.

Macrobius

When we speak of the efficient cause of the universe, we mean, obviously the active Being — the Being active and effective everywhere; we mean, then, that universal Intelligence which appears to be the principal faculty of the World-Soul and, as it were, the general form of the universe.

Giordano Bruno

There is in the universe one power of infinite thought.

Leibnitz

The Idea is cause and end of things.

Giordano Bruno

As one sun illumines all this world, so the conscious Idea illumines all the physical field.

Bhagavad Gita

Matter and Spirit are one since the first beginning.

Ashwaghosha

In the true nature of Matter is the fundamental law of the Spirit. In the true nature of Spirit is the fundamental law of Matter.

Ashwaghosha

He who abases Matter, abases himself and all creation.

Oersted

The physical world is only a reflection of the spiritual.

Antoine the Healer

Wherever you find movement, there you find life and a soul.

Thales

Life pervades and animates everything; it gives its movement to Nature and subjects her to itself.

Giordano Bruno

All is living.

Hermes

The universe is a living thing and all lives in it.

Giordano Bruno

The whole universe is life, force and action.

Giordano Bruno

Each separate movement is produced by the same energy that moves the sum of things.

Hermes

Will is the soul of the universe.

Schopenhauer

In the Beginning

Whence come these beings? What is this creation?

Rig-veda

From the immobile stone to the supreme principle creation consists in the differentiation of existences.

Sankhya Pravachana

Then Non-Being was not, nor Being. What was that ocean profound and impenetrable?

Then death was not, nor immortality.... That was one and lived without the breath by Its own permanence. There was nothing else beyond It.

Darkness concealed in darkness in the beginning was all this ocean.... When chaos atomic covered it, then That which is One was born by the vastness of Its energy.

Desire in the beginning became active, — desire, the first seed....

Who knoweth of this? who here can declare it, whence this creation was born, whence was this loosing forth of things? The gods exist below by the creation; who then can know whence it was born?

Whence this creation came into being, whether He established it or did not establish it, He who regards it from above in the supreme ether, He knows — or perhaps He knows it not.

Rig-veda

That which was before all individual existence, and which was without action although capable of action, is that which preceded heaven and earth.

Huai-nan Tse

Essence without form divided itself;. then a movement took place and life was produced.

Chuang Tse

In the beginning all this was Non-being. From it Being appeared. Itself created itself.

Taittiriya Upanishad

Seek out that from which all existences are born, by which being born they live and to which they return.... From Delight all these existences were born, by Delight they live, towards Delight they return.

Taittiriya Upanishad

The Unknowable Divine

Who knoweth these things? Who can speak of them?

Rig-veda

Things in their fundamental nature can neither be named nor explained. They cannot be expressed adequately in any form of language.

Ashwaghosha

Trying to give an idea of the Ineffable by the help of philosophical learning is like trying to give an idea of Benares by the aid of a map or pictures.

Ramakrishna

All the sacred Scriptures of the world have become corrupted, but the Ineffable or Absolute has never been corrupted, because no one has ever been able to express It in human speech.

Ramakrishna

Words fail us when we seek, not to express Him who Is, but merely to attain to the expression of the powers that environ Him.

Philo

He is pure of all name.

The Bab

The word "He" diminishes Him.

Tolstoy

But call Him by what name you will; for to those who know, He is the possessor of all names.

Baha-ullah

Numerous are the names of the Ineffable and infinite the forms which lead towards Him. Under whatever name or in whatever form you desire to enter into relation with Him, it is in that form and under that name that you will see Him.

Ramakrishna

Would you call Him Destiny? You will not be wrong. Providence? You will say well. Nature? That too you may.

Seneca

The Being that is one, sages speak of in many terms.

Rig-veda

I do not believe that any name, however complex, is sufficient to designate the principle of all Majesty.

Hermes

That which is Permanent, possesses no attribute by which one can speak of It, but the term Permanent is all that can be expressed by language.

Ashwaghosha

The Permanent is neither existence, nor what is at once existence and non-existence; it is neither unity, nor plurality, nor what is at once unity and plurality.

Ashwaghosha

***

Something beyond our power of discrimination existed before Heaven and Earth. How profound is its calm! How absolute its immateriality! It alone exists and does not change; It penetrates all and It does not perish. It may be regarded as the mother of the universe. For myself I know not Its name, but to give it a name I call It Tao.

Lao Tse

There is no suitable name for the eternal Tao.

Lao Tse

The Tao which can be expressed is not the eternal Tao, the name which can be named is not the eternal Name.

Lao Tse

The man who knows the Tao, does not speak; he who speaks, knows It not.

Lao Tse

The eternal Tao has no name; when the Tao divided Itself, then It had a name.

Lao Tse

*
**

If thou say, "Who is the Ancient and most Holy?" come then and see — it is the supreme head, unknowable, inaccessible, indefinable, and it contains all.

Zohar

The name of the Ancient and most Holy is unknowable to all and inaccessible.

Zohar

And it is inaccessible, unknowable and beyond comprehension for all.

Zohar

It is truly the supreme Light, inaccessible and unknowable, from which all other lamps receive their flame and their splendour.

Zohar

*
**

That which has neither body nor appearance, nor form, nor matter, nor can be seized by our senses, That which cannot be expressed — this is God.

Hermes

It is not today nor tomorrow; who knoweth That which is Supreme? When It is approached, It vanishes.

Rig-veda

Is there a single man who can see what the Sage cannot even conceive?

Tseng Tse

No man hath seen God at any time.

John

If he were apparent, He would not be.

Hermes

Yes, His very splendour is the cause of His invisibility.

Baha-ullah

The more thou knowest God, the more thou wilt recognise that thou canst not name Him, nor say what He is.

Angelus Silesius

To comprehend God is difficult, to speak of Him impossible.

Hermes

Thinkest thou that thou canst write the name of God on Time? No more is it pronounced in Eternity.

Angelus Silesius

He who speaks best of God is he who, in the presence of the plenitude of the interior riches, knows best how to be silent.

Eckhart

O Inexpressible, Ineffable, whom silence alone can name!

Hermes

I salute It, this supreme Deity, which is beyond the senses, which mind and speech cannot define and which can be discerned only by the mind of the true sage.

Vishnu Purana

The Divine Essence

If thou canst comprehend God, thou shalt comprehend the Beautiful and the Good, the pure radiance, the incomparable beauty, the good that has not its like.

Hermes

The essence of God, if at all God has an essence, is Beauty.

Hermes

God is Light.

John

He is the supreme Light hidden under every veil.

Zohar

His name is conscious spirit, His abode is conscious spirit and He, the Lord, is all conscious spirit.

Ramakrishna

Knowledge belongs to the very essence of God, if at all God has an essence.

Hermes

God is not knowledge, but the cause of Knowledge; He is not mind, but the cause of mind; He is not Light, but the cause of Light.

Hermes

He is the principle of supreme Wisdom.

Zohar

God is spirit, fire, being and light, and yet He is not all this.

Angelus Silesius

He is an eternal silence.

Angelus Silesius

No name is applicable to God, only He is called Love — so great and precious a thing is Love.

Angelus Silesius

God is Love.

John

Love which overflows on every side, which is found in the centre of the stars, which is in the depths of the Ocean — Love whose perfume declares itself everywhere, which nourishes all the kingdoms of Nature and which maintains equilibrium and harmony in the whole universe.

Antoine the Healer

Victory to the Essence of all wisdom, to the unmoving, to the Imperishable! Victory to the Eternal, to the essence of visible and invisible beings, to Him who is at the same time the cause and the effect of the universe.

Vishnu Purana

He who contemplates the supreme Truth, contemplates the perfect Essence; only the vision of the spirit can see this nature of ineffable perfection.

Japanese Buddhist Meditations

The Divine Becoming

God or the Good, what is it but the existence of that which yet is not?

Hermes

The supreme Brahman without beginning cannot be called either Being or Non-being.

Bhagavad Gita

It is that which is and that which is not.

Hermes

It is Itself that which was and that which is yet to be, the Eternal.

Kaivalya Upanishad

It is He who engenders Himself perpetually — the Lord of existences and of non-existences.

Egyptian Funeral Rites

His creation never had a beginning and will never have an end.

The Bab

Becoming is the mode of activity of the uncreated God.

Hermes

In the bosom of Time God without beginning becomes what He has never been in all eternity.

Angelus Silesius

Time is nothing else than the uninterrupted succession of the acts of divine Energy, one of the attributes or one of the workings of the Deity. Space is the extension of His soul; it is His unfolding in length, breadth and height; it is the simultaneous existence of His productions and manifestations.

Giordano Bruno

As from a fire that is burning brightly sparks of a like nature are produced in their thousands, so from the Unmoving manifold becomings are born and thither also they wend.

Mundaka Upanishad

The Tao is diffused in the universe. All existences return to It as streams and mountain rivulets return to the rivers and the seas.

Lao Tse

Even as the sun rises to us and sets, so also for the creation there are alternations of existence and death.

Harivansha

At the close of the great Night... He whom the spirit alone can perceive, who escapes from the organs of sense, who is without visible parts, Eternal, the soul of all existences, whom none can comprehend, outspread His own splendours.

Laws of Manu

God in All

For what is God? He is the soul of the universe.

Seneca

He is the soul of all conscious creatures, who constitutes all things in this world, those which are beyond our senses and those which fall within their range.

Ashwaghosha

For of all things He is the Lord and Father and Source, and the life and power and light and intelligence and mind.

Hermes

He is everywhere in the world and stands with all in His embrace.

Bhagavad Gita

There is not a body, however small, which does not enclose a portion of the divine substance.

Giordano Bruno

For all is full of God.

Hermes

All this is full of that Being.

Shwetashwatara Upanishad

The fire divine burns indivisible and ineffable and fills all the abysses of the world.

Iamblichus

All the aspects of the sea are not different from the sea; nor is there any difference between the universe and its supreme Principle.

Chhandogya Upanishad

In truth there is no difference between the word of God and the world.

Baha-ullah

God and Nature are one.

Spinoza

That which is most subtle in matter is air, in air the soul, in the soul intelligence, in intelligence God.

Hermes

Material energy in matter, physical energy in the body, essential energy in the essence, all that in its entirety is God and in the universe there is nothing which is not God.

Hermes

In the universe there is nothing which God is not.

Hermes

God is all and all is God.

Eckhart

Heaven and Earth are only a talisman which conceals the Deity; without It they are but a vain name. Know then that the visible world and the invisible are God Himself. There is only He and all that is, is He.

Farid-uddin Attar

He is all things and all things are one.

Zohar

Just as unity is in each of the numbers, so God is one in all things.

Angelus Silesius

All that is one and one that is all.

Hermes

He who is alone uncreated is then by that very fact unrevealed and invisible, but, manifesting all things, He reveals Himself in them and by them.

Hermes

All reflects Him in His shining and by His light all this is luminous.

Katha Upanishad

As the principle of Fire is one, but having entered this world assumes shapes that correspond to each different form, so the one Self in all existences assumes shapes that correspond to each form of things.

Katha Upanishad

He has a form and He is as if He had no form. He has taken a form in order to be the essence of all.

Zohar

The devotee who has seen the One in only one of his aspects, knows Him in that aspect alone. But he who has seen Him in numerous aspects is alone in a position to say, "All these forms are those of the One and the One is multiform." He is without form and in form, and numberless are His forms which we do not know.

Ramakrishna

Such is God, superior to His name, invisible and apparent, who reveals Himself to the spirit, who reveals Himself to the eyes, who has no body and who has many bodies or rather all bodies; for there is nothing which is not He and all is He alone.

Hermes

*
**

God invisible... say not so; for who is more apparent than He? That is the goodness of God, that is His virtue, to be apparent in all.

Hermes

If thou comprehend Him, what seems invisible to most will be for thee utterly apparent.

Hermes

If thou canst, thou mayst see Him by the eyes of the intelligence, for the Lord is not a miser of Himself; He reveals Himself in the whole universe.

Hermes

Thou shalt meet Him everywhere, thou shalt see Him everywhere, in the place and at the hour when thou least expectest it, in waking and in sleep, on the sea, in thy travels, by day, by night, in thy speaking and in thy keeping of silence. For there is nothing that is not the image of God.

Hermes

Raise thyself above every height, descend below every depth, assemble in thyself all the sensations of created things, of water, of fire, of the dry, of the moist; suppose that thou art at once everywhere, on earth, in the sea, in the heavens, that thou wast never born, that thou art still in the womb, that thou art young, old, dead, beyond death; comprehend all at once, times, spaces, things, qualities, and thou shalt comprehend God.

Hermes

Surpass all bodies, traverse all times, become eternity, and thou shalt comprehend God.

Hermes

God in All Beings

The Being whom I declare, is no isolated existence. The whole world is his Being.

Farid-uddin Attar

It is one and the same Being who manifests in all that lives.

Schopenhauer

Individual existences are merely modifications of the divine qualities.

Spinoza

Every man whose heart is free from the perturbations of doubt, knows with certitude that there is no being save One alone. The word "I" belongs rightly to none but God.

Gulschen-i-Raz

There is one self in all existences which appears as if different in different creatures.

Amritabindu Upanishad

The one God hidden in all beings who pervades all things and is the inner Self of all creatures, who presides over all actions and dwells in all existences.

Shwetashwatara Upanishad

He who abiding in the mind is inward to mind, whom the mind knows not, of whom mind is the body, who within governs the mind, He is thy Self and inward guide and immortal.

Brihadaranyaka Upanishad

Without being divided in creatures It dwells in them as if divided.

Bhagavad Gita

*
**

He sees rightly who beholds the supreme Lord dwelling equally in all existences and not perishing when they perish.

Bhagavad Gita

Things in their fundamental nature are subject neither to transformation nor to destruction. They are all one single soul.

Ashwaghosha

It is not the individuals visible to us who are modified, it is the universal substance which is modified in each of them. And to that substance what other name shall we give but first substance? It is this which is and becomes. It is the eternal God, and we err when we forget His name and form and see only the names and forms of each individual.

Apollonius

And these bodies that end are of an eternal soul, indestructible and immeasurable, unborn, everlasting, ancient, all-pervading, stable, immobile, not manifest, beyond thought, immutable — as such it should be known.

Bhagavad Gita

Since it is without beginning or quality, this supreme Self, imperishable though residing in the body, . . . is situated everywhere and remains in the body untouched and unstained.

Bhagavad Gita

*
* *

One soul is distributed among all unreasoning existences, one intelligent soul is shared by all beings that have reason.

Marcus Aurelius

For there is one world formed of all, one God pervading all, one substance, one Law, one Reason common to all intelligent beings.

Marcus Aurelius

What is Reason? It is a portion of the divine Spirit that is diffused in our bodies.

Seneca

It is the Spirit that is in men, it is the breath of the Almighty that gives them understanding.

Job

He is the intelligence in every living creature.

Brihadaranyaka Upanishad

God in Each

I am the Self who abides in the heart of all beings.

Bhagavad Gita

I am the beginning, the middle and the end of all existences.

Bhagavad Gita

Turn thy regard on thyself that thou mayst find Me erect within thee.

Baha-ullah

Who is so low that one can see all His aspects? Who is so high that one cannot attain to Him? The One concealed whose name is unknown! He is among men and close to the gods, when they live and when they die. Without cessation He holds their existence in His hand. They are in Him eternally.

Hymn to Ptah

He who is here in man and He who is there in the Sun, is the same.

Taittiriya Upanishad

The Lord who is established in the secret place of every soul, pervades the whole universe.

Shwetashwatara Upanishad

He is the Light of all lights that is beyond the darkness; He is the knowledge and the object of knowledge and its goal and dwells in the heart of all.

Bhagavad Gita

The Lord dwells in the heart of all beings and He turns all of them as upon a machine by His Maya.

Bhagavad Gita

The jewel of the perfect nature clear and luminous as the sun dwells in every being.

Japanese Buddhist Meditations

This is that truth and immortality in which all the worlds and their creatures are established; this know for the supreme aim.

Mundaka Upanishad

In all hearts dwells the shining One, so have the sages declared.

Guru Granth Sahib

Now life has this sense, that as our consciousness becomes more and more clear, it discloses in us God.

Tolstoy

Yes, we need a new revelation, not about Hell and Heaven, but the spirit which lives in us.

Channing

Let man then learn the revelation of all Nature and all thought to his heart; this, namely, that the Highest dwells with him, that the sources of Nature are in his own mind.

Emerson

The Light that shines most high of all, higher than every other thing, in the highest world beyond which there is no other, is the same light that is in man.

Chhandogya Upanishad

Its name is the God in man.

Lao Tse

The soul of every man contains God in potentiality.

Vivekananda

The seed of the Divinity is planted in our bodies.

Seneca

He is called the supreme self in this body and the supreme Soul.

Bhagavad Gita

A holy spirit dwells in our soul.

Seneca

The soul and self within established in the heart of man.

Shwetashwatara Upanishad

God is not where we believe Him to be; He is in ourselves.

Antoine the Healer

The Kingdom of Heaven is within us.

Luke

For the throne of God is in our hearts, His kingdom is within us.

Tauler

He himself is within us, so that we are His vessels, His living temples, His incarnations.

Epictetus

We are the temple of the living God.

Corinthians

Know you not that you are the temple of God and the Spirit of God dwelleth in you?

Corinthians

Know you not that your body is the temple of the Holy Ghost which is in you?

Corinthians

God is not remote from you, He is with you and in you.

Seneca

You are yourselves He whom you seek.

Vivekananda

He Is Thyself

Why should man go about seeking God? He is in thy heart-beats and thou knowest it not; thou wert in error in seeking Him outside thyself.

Vivekananda

He who finds not the Eternal in himself, will never find it outside; but he who sees Him in the temple of his own soul, sees Him also in the temple of the universe.

Ramakrishna

Where wouldst thou seek God? Seek Him in thy soul which is eternal in its nature and contains the divine birth.

Boehme

Heaven is within thee. If thou seek God elsewhere, thou wilt never find Him.

Angelus Silesius

God cannot be recognised except in oneself. So long as thou findest Him not in thee, thou wilt not find Him anywhere. There is no God for the man who does not feel Him in himself.

Tolstoy

Thou shouldst not cry after God: the Source is in thyself.

Angelus Silesius

While thou art saying "I am alone with myself," in thy heart there is dwelling uninterruptedly that supreme Spirit, silent observer of all good and all evil.

Laws of Manu

Thou seest Him, yet thou knowest not that thou seest.

Mohyuddin ibn Arabi

Thou are not, but only He.

Mohyuddin ibn Arabi

Thou art He and He is thou.

Mohyuddin ibn Arabi

This supreme Brahman, the self of all, the great abode of the universe, more subtle than the subtle, eternal, That is thyself and thou art That.

Kaivalya Upanishad

Thou art That... not a part, not a mode of It, but identically That, the absolute Spirit.

Chhandogya Upanishad

All the attributes of Allah are thy attributes.

Mohyuddin ibn Arabi

The essence of our being, the mystery in us which calls itself "I", — what words have we to express things like these? It is a breath of Heaven; the Highest reveals itself in man. This body, these faculties, this life that we live, is it not all a robe for Him who is nameless?

Carlyle

The doctrine of this supreme Presence is a cry of joy and exaltation. What man seeing this can lose it from his thought or entertain a meaner subject?

Emerson

The greatest joy man can conceive is the joy of recognising in himself a being free, intelligent, loving and in consequence happy, of feeling God in himself.

Tolstoy

*
**

Man in order to be really a man must conceive the idea of God in himself.

Tolstoy

The individual "I" and the supreme Spirit are one and the same. The difference is in degree: the one is finite, the other infinite; the one is dependent, the other independent.

Ramakrishna

Man ought always to say in his thought, I am God Himself.

Upanishad

God is my inmost self, the reality of my being.

Vivekananda

God is myself; we are one in consciousness and His knowing is my knowing.

Eckhart

The Purusha who is there and there, He am I.

Isha Upanishad

If I were not, God would not be.

Eckhart

I know that I have in me something without which nothing could be. It is that I call God.

Angelus Silesius

They regarded the divine Being and grew assured that it was no other than themselves... that they were themselves that Being... that they and that Being made but one.

Farid-uddin Attar

So Should He Be Adored

So should He be adored...for it is in That all become one.

Brihadaranyaka Upanishad

Hail to Thee, to Thee, Spirit of the Supreme Spirit, Soul of souls, to Thee, the visible and invisible, who art one with Time and with the elements.

Vishnu Purana

O obscurity of obscurity, O soul of the soul, Thou art more than all and before all. All is seen in Thee and Thou art seen in all.

Farid-uddin Attar

I see of Thee neither end nor middle nor beginning, O Lord of all and universal form.

Bhagavad Gita

First of the elements, universal Being, Thou hast created all and preservest all and the universe is nothing but Thy form.

Vishnu Purana

Sole essence of the world, Thou createst it and Thou dissolvest it. Thou makest and unmakest the universe which is born again unceasingly by Thee.

Harivansha

When creation perishes, Thou dost not perish, when it is reborn, thou coverest it, O Imperishable, with a thousand different forms.

Harivansha

Thou art the sun, the stars, the planets, the entire world, all that is without form or endowed with form, all that is visible or invisible, Thou art all these.

Vishnu Purana

Thou art also in the trees and the plants; the earth bears Thee in its flanks and gives birth to Thee as its nursling, Thee, the Lord of beings, Thee, the essence of all that exists.

Harivansha

Whither shall I go from Thy spirit or whither shall I flee from Thy presence? If I ascend up into heaven, Thou art there; if I make my bed in hell, behold Thou art there.

Psalms

Where shall I direct my gaze to bless Thee, on high, below, without, within? There is no way, no place that is outside Thee, other beings exist not; all is in Thee.

Hermes

Thou who art the soul of all things, Thy universal diffusion witnesses to Thy power and goodness. It is in thee, in others, in all creatures, in all worlds.

Vishnu Purana

All that is contains Thee; I could not exist if Thou wert not in me.

St. Augustine

I have strayed like a lost sheep seeking outside me that which was within. I have run about the streets and places of the world, this great city, seeking Thee and I have not found Thee because I sought Thee ill and came not to the place where Thou wert. Thou wert within me and I sought Thee without; Thou wert near and I sought Thee at a distance, and if I had gone where Thou wert, I should immediately have met Thee.

St. Augustine

Thou art all that I can be, Thou art all that I can do, Thou art all that I can say; for Thou art all and there is nothing that Thou art not. Thou art all that is and all that yet is not.

Hermes

Master invisible, filling all hearts and directing them from within, to whatever side I look, Thou dwellest there.

Bharon Guru

Thou art the sovereign treasure of this universe.

Bhagavad Gita

Through Thy creations I have discovered the beatitude of Thy eternity.

Hermes

To Become God in Order to Know Him

Only the like knows its like.

Porphyry

God dwells in a Light, to which a road is wanting. He who does not become That himself, will never see It.

Angelus Silesius

What God is one knows not. He is not light, nor spirit, nor beatitude, nor unity, nor what goes by the name of divinity, nor wisdom, nor love, nor will, nor kindness, nor a thing, nor that which is not a thing, nor a being, nor a soul; He is what neither I nor thou nor any creature will ever know until we have become what He is.

Angelus Silesius

For nobody can see what He is, except the soul in which He himself is.

Eckhart

Lose thyself in Him to penetrate this mystery; everything else is superfluous.

Farid-uddin Attar

Do not think to gain God by thy actions.... One must not gain but be God.

Angelus Silesius

One must be God in order to understand God.

Antoine the Healer

If thou canst not equal thyself with God, thou canst not understand Him.

Hermes

Be not astonished that man can become like God.

Epistle to Diognetius

If man surrenders himself to Tao, he identifies himself with Tao.

Lao Tse

Whoever thinks himself an imperfect and worldly soul, is really an imperfect and worldly soul; whoever deems himself divine, becomes divine. What a man thinks he is, he becomes.

Ramakrishna

That is why it is permitted to him who has attained to the truth within to say, "I am the true Divine."

Mohyuddin ibn Arabi

Become what thou art.

Orphic Precept

Each man ought to say to himself, "I was the creator, may I become again what I was."

Upanishad

Before I was myself, I was God in God, that is why I can again become that when I shall be dead to myself.

Angelus Silesius

The Gods

He who knows that He is the supreme Lord, becomes that, and the gods themselves cannot prevent him.... He who adores any other divinity, has not the knowledge. He is as cattle for the gods. Even as numerous cattle serve to nourish men, so each man serves to nourish the gods.... That is why the gods love not that a man should know That.

Brihadaranyaka Upanishad

And the Lord Jehovah said, "Behold, the man is become as one of us...and now, lest he put forth his hand, and take also of the tree of life, and eat, and live forever, therefore the Lord God sent him forth from the garden of Eden."

Genesis

The belief in supernatural beings may to a certain extent increase the action in man, but it produces also a moral deterioration. Dependence, fear, superstition accompany it; it degenerates into a miserable belief in the weakness of man.

Vivekananda

Man is the creator of the gods whom he worships in his temples. Therefore humanity has made its gods in its own image.

Hermes

The Ancestors fashioned the gods as a workman fashions iron.

Rig-veda

Little children, keep yourselves from idols.

John

For we wrestle not against flesh and blood, but against principalities, against powers, against the rulers of the darkness of this world, against spiritual wickedness in high places.

Ephesians

For though there be that are called gods, whether in heaven or in earth (as there be gods

many and lords many), but to us there is but one
God, of whom are all things.

Corinthians

All is full of gods.

Thales

All the gods and goddesses are only varied
aspects of the One.

Ramakrishna

The gods have been created by Him, but of
Him who knows the manner of His being?

Rig-veda

We should not make comparisons between
the gods. When a man has really seen a divinity,
he knows that all divinities are manifestations of
one and the same Brahman.

Ramakrishna

That is worlds, gods, beings, the All — the
supreme Soul.

Brihadaranyaka Upanishad

The Divine Man

Ye are Gods.

Psalms

None of the heavenly gods quits his sphere to come upon the earth, while man mounts up to heaven and measures it. He knows what is on high and what is below. He knows all correctly and, what is more, has no need to leave the earth in order to exalt himself.

Hermes

None is greater than he. The gods themselves will have to descend upon earth and it is in a human form that they will get their salvation. Man alone reaches the perfection of which the gods themselves are ignorant.

Vivekananda

What is man?... Thou crownedst him with glory and honour,... thou hast put all things in subjection under his feet.

Hebrews

By the assemblage of all that is exalted and all that is base man was always the most astonishing of mysteries.

Farid-uddin Attar

The world is full of marvels and the greatest marvel is man.

Sophocles

Man is a small universe.

Democritus

Placed on the borders of Time and Eternity ... he holds himself somehow erect at the horizon of Nature.... Spiritual perfection is his true destiny.

Giordano Bruno

He is the king of Nature because he alone in the world knows himself.... His substance is that of God Himself.

The Rose of Bakanali

Heaven and Earth are the father and mother of all beings; among beings man alone has intelligence for his portion.

Shu Ching

It is we who, in the eyes of Intelligence, are the essence of the divine regard.

Omar Khayyam

That Intelligence is God within us; by that men are gods and their humanity neighbours divinity.

Hermes

Man is divine so long as he is in communion with the Eternal.

Ramakrishna

Deck thyself now with majesty and excellence and array thyself with glory and beauty.

Job

Thou belongest to the divine world.

Baha-ullah

The race of men is divine.

Pythagoras

*
**

One should seek God among men.

Novalis

Follow the great man and you will see what the world has at heart in these ages. There is no omen like that.

Emerson

There is always one man who more than others represents the divine thought of the epoch.

Emerson

A link was wanting between two craving parts of Nature and he was hurled into being as the bridge over that yawning need.

Emerson

There is only one temple in the universe and that is the body of man. Nothing is holier than this noble form. To bow down before man is a homage offered to this revelation in the flesh. We touch heaven when we lay our hand on a human body.

Novalis

Within man is the soul of the whole, the wise silence, the universal beauty to which every part and particle is equally related, the eternal One.

Emerson

BOOK TWO

THE DISCOVERY AND CONQUEST
OF THE DIVINE IN ONESELF

SECTION I

THE CONQUEST OF TRUTH

The Aspiration towards Truth

When darkness envelops you, do you not seek for a lamp?

Dhammapada

Man finds himself a centre of Nature, his fragment of Time surrounded by Eternity, his span of Space surrounded by Infinity. How can he help asking himself, "What am I? and whence have I come and whither do I go?"

Carlyle

This world after all our sciences remains still a miracle, marvellous, inscrutable, magical and more, for whoever thinks.

Carlyle

One beholds it as a mystery, another speaks of it as a mystery, another learns of it as a mystery and even when one has learned of it, there is none that knows it.

Bhagavad Gita

And yet, O the happiness of being man and of being able to recognise the way of the Truth and by following it to attain the goal.

Gyokai

The supreme gift is the gift of Truth, the supreme savour is the savour of Truth, the supreme delight is the delight of Truth.

Dhammapada

Awake, arise, strive incessantly towards the knowledge so that thou mayst attain unto the peace.

Buddhist Text

True royalty consists in spiritual knowledge; turn thy efforts to its attainment.

Farid-uddin Attar

The man who does not try to raise his spirit above itself, is not worthy to live in the condition of a man.

Angelus Silesius

Seek and ye shall find.

Matthew

To the eyes of men athirst the whole world seems in dream as a spring of water.

Saadi

Ho, every one that thirsteth, come ye to the waters, and he that hath no money...come, buy wine and milk without money and without price.... Incline your ear and come, hear and your soul shall live.

Isaiah

O children of immortality, you who live on the highest summits, the road is found, there is a way to escape out of the shadow; and this means, the soul — for there are no others — is to perceive Him who is beyond all darkness.

Vivekananda

To look on high, to learn what is beyond, to seek to raise oneself always.

Pasteur

**

I will lift up mine eyes unto the hills from whence cometh my help!

Psalms

Heaven is my father and begot me; I have for my family all this heavenly circle. My mother is the boundless earth. But I know not to what all this mysterious universe is like, my eyes are troubled and I move as if enchained in my own thought.

Rig-veda

I invoke the excellent people of the stars of pure knowledge, pure greatness and beneficent light.

Zend-Avesta

I desire and love nothing that is not of the light.

Zend-Avesta

To my eyes the majesty of lords and princes is only a little smoke that floats in a ray of sunlight.

Sutra in Forty-two Articles

To my eyes treasures, diamonds and precious stones are as mere charcoal and coarseness; to my eyes cloth of silk and brocades of price are but rags and tatters.

Sutra in Forty-two Articles

I renounce the honours to which the world aspires and desire only to know the Truth.

Socrates

Always higher must I mount, higher must I see.

Goethe

What has been said about God, is still not enough for me; the supra-divine is my life and my light.

Angelus Silesius

O Thou who hast hidden thyself behind a veil, withdraw that veil at last, so that my soul may not consume itself in the search for Thee.

Farid-uddin Attar

When thou saidst, Seek ye my face, my heart said unto Thee, Thy face, Lord, will I seek.

Psalms

With my soul have I desired thee in the night; with my spirit within me will I seek thee early.

Isaiah

In that God who illumines the reason, desiring liberation I seek my refuge.

Shwetashwatara Upanishad

I will rise now and go about the city in the streets and the broadways, I will seek him whom my soul loveth.

Song of Songs

Verily, I say to thee; he who seeks the Eternal, finds Him.

Ramakrishna

He who seeks him, finds him; he who yearns intensely after the Ineffable, has found the Ineffable.

Ramakrishna

O son of earth, be blind and thou shalt see My beauty; be deaf and thou shalt hear My sweet song, My pleasant melody; be ignorant and thou shalt partake My knowledge; be in distress and thou shalt have an eternal portion of the infinite ocean of My riches: — blind to all that is not My beauty, deaf to all that is not My word, ignorant of all that is not My knowledge. Thus with a gaze that is pure, a spirit without stain, an understanding refined, thou shalt enter into my sacred presence.

Baha-ullah

Wide open to all beings be the gates of the Everlasting.

Mahavagga

The Quest Within

The sage's quest is for himself, the quest of the ignorant for other than himself.

Confucius

Nobility is for each man within him; only he never thinks of seeking for it within.

Meng Tse

If anyone asks what is the shortest and surest way of disposing ourselves to advance continually in the spiritual life, I shall reply that it is to remain carefully self-gathered within, for it is there properly that one sees the gleam of the true light.

Tauler

To retire from the world, that is to retire into oneself, is to aid in the dispersion of all doubts.

Tolstoy

If the soul would give itself leisure to take breath and return into itself, it would be easy for it to draw from its own depths the seeds of the true.

Seneca

Assuredly, whoever wishes to discover the universal truth must sound the depths of his own heart.

Tauler

Only from his own soul can he demand the secret of eternal beauty.

Farid-uddin Attar

**

Examine yourselves.

II Corinthians

Your greatness is within and only in yourselves can you find a spectacle worthy of your regard.

Seneca

Seek and you shall find.... It is when we seek for the things which are within us that quest leads to discovery.

Meng Tse

Our true glory and true riches are within.

Seneca

Of what use is it to run painfully about the troubled world of visible things when there is a purer world within ourselves?

Novalis

The soul will enjoy veritable felicity when, separating itself from the darkness which surrounds it, it is able to contemplate with a sure gaze the divine light at its source.

Seneca

Each descent of the gaze on oneself is at the same time an ascension, an assumption, a gaze on the true objectivity.

Novalis

I looked into my own heart and I saw reflected there in its entirety the vast world with all its passions — pride, hope, fear and the conflagration of the desires. So gazing I understood the word of the ancient sage, "Man is a mirror in which there appears the image of the world."

Ryonin

*
**

The day of days, the great feast-day of the life, is that in which the eye within opens on the unity of things, the omnipresence of a law.

Emerson

The law is not in heaven that thou shouldst say, "Who shall go up for us to heaven and bring it into us that we may hear it and do it?" Neither is it beyond the sea, that thou shouldst say, "Who shall go over the sea and bring it into us that we may hear it and do it?" But the word is very nigh unto thee, in thy mouth and in thy heart, that thou mayst do it.

Deuteronomy

Observe thyself, not that which is thine, nor that which is around thee, but thyself alone.

St. Basil

Retire into thyself as into an island and set thyself to the work.

Dhammapada

Gather thyself into thyself crouched like an infant in the bosom of its mother.

Farid-uddin Attar

Look within thee; within thee is the source of all good and a source inexhaustible provided thou dig in it unceasingly.

Marcus Aurelius

Contemplate the mirror of thy heart and thou shalt taste little by little a pure joy and unmixed peace.

Saadi

Open the eye of the heart that thou mayst see thy soul; thou shalt see what was not made to be seen.

Ahmed Halif

The soul is veiled by the body; God is veiled by the soul.

Farid-uddin Attar

If a man could cast a firm and clear glance into the depths of his being, he would see there God.

Tauler

Every man who returns into himself will find there traces of the Divinity.

Cicero

Look into thy heart and thou shalt see there His image.

Farid-uddin Attar

An attentive scrutiny of thy being will reveal to thee that it is one with the very essence of absolute perfection.

Japanese Buddhist Writings

O my friend, hearken to the melody of the Spirit in thy heart and in thy soul and guard it as the apple of thy eyes.

Baha-ullah

But how can that be manifested to thy eyes if what is within thee is to thyself invisible?

Hermes

This Self hidden in all existences shines not out, but it is seen with the supreme and subtle vision by those who see the subtle. The wise man should draw speech into the mind, mind into the Self that is knowledge; knowledge he should contain in the Great Self and that in the Self that is still.

Katha Upanishad

Let not him then who cannot enter into the chamber of hidden treasure complain that he is poor and has no part in these riches.

Tauler

What right has a man to say he has a soul if he has not felt it or that there is a God if he has not seen Him? If we have a soul, we must penetrate to it; otherwise it is better not to believe, to be frankly an atheist rather than a hypocrite.

Vivekananda

O my soul, wilt thou be one day simple, one, bare, more visible than the body which envelops thee?

Marcus Aurelius

Know Thyself

Know thyself and thou shalt know the universe and the gods.

Inscription of the Temple of Delphi

One of the most important precepts of wisdom is to know oneself.

Socrates

There is nothing greater than the practice of the precept which says, "Know thyself."

Antoine the Healer

The sage knows himself.

Lao Tse

All men participate in the possibility of self-knowledge.

Heraclitus

Let the man in whom there is intelligence ...know himself.

Hermes

Let each contemplate himself, not shut up in narrow walls, not cabined in a corner of the earth, but a citizen of the whole world. From the height of the sublime meditations which the spectacle of Nature and the knowledge of it will procure for him, how well will he know himself! how he will disdain, how base he will find all the futilities to which the vulgar attach so high a price.

Cicero

When one says to a man, "Know thyself," it is not only to lower his pride, but to make him sensible of his own value.

Cicero

Ignorance of oneself is then an evil in all respects, whether ignoring the greatness and dignity of the inner man one lowers one's divine principle or ignoring the natural baseness of the external man one commits the fault of glorifying oneself.

Porphyry

*
**

The supreme task of culture is to take possession of one's transcendental self, to be truly the self of the self.... Without a complete intelligence of oneself one will never learn to understand others aright.

Novalis

If then we wish to give ourselves to the study of philosophy, let us apply ourselves to self-knowledge and we shall arrive at a right philosophy by elevating ourselves from the conception of ourselves to the contemplation of the universe.

Porphyry

Whoever wishes to attain to the highest perfection of his being and to the vision of the supreme good, must have a knowledge of himself as of the things about him to the very core. It is only so that he can arrive at the supreme clarity. Therefore learn to know thyself, that is better for thee than to know all the powers of the creation.

Eckhart

Whoever knows himself, has light.

Lao Tse

Whoever knows essentially his own nature, can know also that of other men and can penetrate into the nature of things. He can collaborate in the transformations and in the progress of heaven and of earth.

Confucius

How can the soul which misunderstands itself have a sure idea of other creatures?

Seneca

The soul of man is the mirror of the world.

Leibnitz

The soul is the image of what is above it and the model of what is below. Therefore by knowing and analysing itself it knows all things without going out of its own nature.

Proclus

The soul includes everything; whoever knows his soul, knows everything and whoever is ignorant of his soul, is ignorant of everything.

Socrates

This mental being in the inner heart who has the truth and the light is the lord and sovereign of all; he who knows it, governs all this that is.

Brihadaranyaka Upanishad

Whoever develops all the faculties of his thinking principle, knows his own rational nature; once he knows his rational nature, he knows heaven.

Meng Tse

The greatest science is the knowledge of oneself. He who knows himself, knows God.

St. Clement of Alexandria

As by knowing one piece of clay one knows all that is of clay, as by knowing one implement of steel one knows all that is of steel, even so is the order of this knowledge.

Chhandogya Upanishad

He who knows himself, knows his Lord.

Mohyuddin ibn Arabi

Know thyself and thou shalt know the Non-ego and the Lord of all. Meditate deeply, thou shalt find there is nothing thou canst call "I". The innermost result of all analysis is the eternal divine. When egoism vanishes, divinity manifests itself.

Ramakrishna

When thou takest cognizance of what thine "I" is, then art thou delivered from egoism and shalt know that thou art not other than God.

Mohyuddin ibn Arabi

When thou canst see that the substance of His being is thy being... then thou knowest thy soul.... So to know oneself is the true knowledge.

Mohyuddin ibn Arabi

The zeal we devote to fulfilling the precept "Know thyself," leads us to the true happiness whose condition is the knowledge of veritable truths.

Porphyry

It is written in the great Law, "Before thou canst become a knower of the All-Self, thou must first be the knower of thine own self."

Book of the Golden Precepts

Who knows this ruler within, he knows the worlds and the gods and creatures and the Self, he knows all.

Brihadaranyaka Upanishad

That is the bright Light of all lights which they know who know themselves.

Mundaka Upanishad

He becomes master of all this universe who has this knowledge.

Brihadaranyaka Upanishad

Know thyself, sound the divinity.

Epictetus

The Paths of Understanding

Love light and not darkness.

Orphic Hymns

The light shineth in the darkness and the darkness comprehendeth it not.... It was in the world and the world was made by it, and the world knew it not.

John

Comprehend then the light and know it.

Hermes

The whole dignity of man is in thought. Labour then to think aright.

Pascal

Our inner self is provided with all necessary faculties.

Meng Tse

The spirit constructs its own abode; directed falsely from the beginning it thinks in erroneous ways and engenders its own distress. Thought creates for itself its own suffering.

Fa-ken-pi-u

Not only to unite oneself by the breath to the air in which we live, but henceforth to unite oneself by thought to the Intelligence in which all lives. For intelligent Power is no less diffused everywhere and is no less communicated to whoever can breathe it.

Marcus Aurelius

You tell me that even in Europe educated men become mad by thinking constantly of one subject. But how is it possible to lose one's intelligence and become mad by thinking of that Intelligence by which the whole world is made intelligent?

Ramakrishna

The law of the grand study or practical philosophy consists in developing and bringing into light the luminous principle of reason which we have received from heaven.

Confucius

Reason is the foundation of all things.

Li Chi

In the beginning all things were in confusion; intelligence came and imposed order.

Anaxagoras

Intelligence, soul divine, truly dominates all — destiny, law and everything else.

Hermes

To it nothing is impossible, neither to place the soul above destiny nor to submit it to destiny by rendering it indifferent to circumstances. Nothing is more divine or more powerful than Intelligence.

Hermes

We believe often that the greatest force existent in the world is material force. We so think because our body, whether we will or no, feels always that force. But spiritual force, the force of thought seems to us insignificant and we do not recognise it as a force at all. Nevertheless it is there that true force resides, that which modifies our life and the life of others.

Tolstoy

Force cannot resist intelligence; in spite of force, in spite of men, intelligence passes on and triumphs.

Ramakrishna

There is nothing in the world that man's intelligence cannot attain, annihilate or accomplish.

Hindu Saying

Beware when the Almighty sends a thinker on this planet; all is then in peril.

Emerson

Intelligence is worth more than all the possessions in the world.

Minokhired

It is nothing, O my brothers, the loss of relatives, riches or honours; but the loss of understanding is a heavy loss. It is nothing, O my brothers, the gain of relatives, riches or honours; but the gain of understanding is the supreme gain. Therefore we wish to gain in understanding; let that be our aspiration.

Anguttara Nikaya

Thou shalt call Intelligence by the name of mother.

Kabbalah

Intelligence is the beneficent guide of human souls, it leads them towards their good.

Hermes

The great malady of the soul is error which brings in its train all evils without any good. Intelligence combats it and brings back the soul to good as the physician restores the body to health.

Hermes

Cultivate the intelligence so that you may drink of the torrent of certitude.

Baha-ullah

Strive to understand with that supreme intuition which will cause you to attain to divine knowledge and which is in harmony with the soul of eternal things, so that the mysteries of spiritual wisdom may be clearly revealed to you.

Baha-ullah

Man should never cease to believe that the incomprehensible can be comprehended; otherwise he would give up his search.

Goethe

Our intelligence arrives by application at the understanding and knowledge of the nature of the world. The understanding of the nature of the world arrives at the knowledge of the eternal.

Hermes

For the spirit searcheth all things, yea, the deep things of God.

I Corinthians

Man's vast spirit in its power to understand things, has a wider extent than heaven and earth.

Tauler

Try, but thou shalt not find the frontiers of the soul even if thou scourest all its ways; so profound is the extension of its reasoning being.

Heraclitus

The Spirit of Synthesis

To think is to move in the Infinite.

Lacordaire

Wouldst thou penetrate the infinite? Advance, then, on all sides in the finite.

Goethe

There is one height of truth and there are those who approach from all sides, as many sides as there are radii in a circle, that is to say, by routes of an infinite variety. Let us work, then, with all our strength to arrive at this light of Truth which unites us all.

Tolstoy

All is truth for the intellect and reason.

Hermes

As the musician knows how to tune his lyre, so the wise man knows how to set his mind in tune with all minds.

Demophilus

If faith and incredulity offered themselves together to him, he would receive them with an equal willingness, let them but open to him the door through which he must pass to his goal.

Farid-uddin Attar

One must receive the Truth from wheresoever it may come.

Maimonides

Accept what is good even from the babbling of an idiot or the prattle of a child as they extract gold from a stone.

Mahabharata

Seek the Truth, though you must go to China to find it.

Mohammed

When they tell thee that thou must not search everywhere for truth, believe them not. Those who speak thus are thy most formidable enemies — and Truth's.

Tolstoy

Examine all things and hold fast that which is good.

St. Paul

Behind each particular idea there is a general idea, an absolute principle. Know that and you know all.

Vivekananda

Contraries harmonise with each other; the finest harmony springs from things that are unlike.

Heraclitus

Whoever would enter into the mysteries of Nature must incessantly explore the opposite extremes of things and discover the point where they unite.

Giordano Bruno

The more we rise towards the summit, towards the identity, both through the form and in the essence, and the more we turn away from particular things towards the whole, the more do we find the unity that abides for ever and behold it as supreme, dominant, comprehensive of diversity and multiplicity.

Iamblichus

The more our reason adopts the ways and processes of this sovereign Reason which is at once that which knows and that which is known, the better are we enabled to understand the totality of things. Whosoever sees and possesses this unity, possesses all; whoever has been unable to reach this unity, has grasped nothing.

Giordano Bruno

The Purification of the Mind

There is a stain worse than all stains, the stain of ignorance. Purify yourselves of that stain, O disciples, and be free from soil.

Dhammapada

The plague of ignorance overflows all the earth.

Hermes

Men and women live in the world without yet having any idea either of the visible world or the invisible.

Farid-uddin Attar

Man is like an ignorant spectator of a drama played on the stage.

Bhagavata Purana

The ignorant is a child.

Laws of Manu

Ignorance is the night of the spirit, but a night without stars or moon.

Chinese Proverb

Ignorance is the field in which all other difficulties grow.

Patanjali

The evil of the soul is ignorance.

Hermes

Ignorance is almost always on the point of doing evil.

Chinese Proverb

With ignorance are born all the passions, with the destruction of ignorance the passions also are destroyed.

Majjhima Nikaya

There is in this world no purification like knowledge.

Bhagavad Gita

Even though thou shouldst be of all sinners the most sinful, yet by the raft of knowledge thou shalt cross utterly beyond all evil.

Bhagavad Gita

Fill then your heart with this knowledge and seek for the sources of life in the words dictated by Truth itself.

Epistle to Diognetus

There is a ceremony which is called the baptism of the purification. It is celebrated with solemnity and pomp, but it is not the true purification. I will teach you that noble baptism which leads to deliverance.

Sanyutta Nikaya

It is not by the water in which they plunge that men become pure but he becomes pure who follows the path of the Truth.

Sanyutta Nikaya

And ye shall know the truth and the truth shall make you free.

St. John

Behold, my son, the plenitude of the good which follows the appearance of the Truth, for envy removes far from us and by the truth the good arrives with life and light and there no longer remain in us any executioners or darkness; all withdraw vanquished.

Hermes

But most men, I know not why, love better to deceive themselves and fight obstinately for an opinion which is to their taste than to seek without obduracy the truth.

Cicero

We have no power against the truth, we have power only for the truth.

II Corinthians

Happy are they whom Truth herself instructs not by words and figures but by showing herself as she is.

Thomas à Kempis

Truth is the perfect virtue, the sovereign good that is not troubled by matter nor circumscribed by the body, the good, bare, evident, unalterable, august, immutable.

Hermes

Regard as true only the eternal and the just.

Hermes

The True Science

The knowledge which purifies the intelligence is true knowledge. All the rest is ignorance.

Ramakrishna

He alone is truly a man who is illumined by the light of the true knowledge. Others are only men in name.

Ramakrishna

Human opinions are playthings.

Heraclitus

Those, on the contrary, who contemplate the immutable essence of things, have knowledge and not opinions.

Plato

To know is not to be well informed; it is our own effort that must reveal all to us and we can owe nothing to other than ourselves.

Antoine the Healer

It is difficult, even after having learned much, to arrive at the desired term of science.

Sutra in Forty-two Articles

Whoever has perfected himself by the spiritual union, finds in time the true science in himself.

Bhagavad Gita

Just discernment is of two kinds. The first conducts us towards the phenomenon, while the second knows how the Absolute appears in the universe.

Ramakrishna

The experimental sciences, when one occupies oneself with them for their own sake, studying them without any philosophical aim, are like a face without eyes. They then represent one of those occupations suitable to middling capacities devoid of the supreme gifts which would only be obstacles to their minute researches.

Schopenhauer

When a man has studied all sciences and learned what men know and have known, he will find that all these sciences taken as a whole are so insignificant that they bring with them no possibility of understanding the world.

Tolstoy

The observations and reckonings of astronomers have taught us many surprising things, but the most important result of their studies is, undoubtedly, that they reveal to us the abyss of our ignorance.

Kant

There is no fact in Science which may not tomorrow be turned into ridicule.... The very hopes of man, the thoughts of his heart, the religions of the peoples, the customs and ethics of humanity are all at the mercy of a new generalisation. The generalisation is always a new current of the divine in the spirit.

Emerson

We must distinguish between the knowledge which is due to the study and analysis of Matter and that which results from contact with life and a benevolent activity in the midst of humanity.

Antoine the Healer

The young generations study numberless subjects, the constitution of the stars, of the earth, the origin of organisms, etc. They omit only one thing and that is to know what is the sense of human life, how one ought to live, what the great sages of all times have thought of this question and how they have resolved it.

Tolstoy

For life cannot subsist without science and science exposes us to this peril that it does not walk towards the light of the true life.

Epistle to Diognetus

Save the world that is within us, O Life.

Hermes

Whoever, without having the true science to which Life offers witness, fancies he knows something, knows, I repeat, nothing.

Epistle to Diognetus

Let no man deceive himself; if any man among you seemeth to be wise in this world, let him become a fool that he may be wise.

I Corinthians

If thou wouldst make progress, be resigned to passing for an idiot or an imbecile in external things; consent to pass for one who understands nothing of them at all.

Epictetus

The sage is not a savant nor the savant a sage.

Lao Tse

Out of academies there come more fools than from any other class in society.

Kant

The knowledge of a great number of trivialities is an insurmountable obstacle to knowing what is really necessary.

Tolstoy

Take care that the reading of numerous writers and books of all kinds does not confuse and trouble thy reason.

Seneca

It would be better not to have books than to believe all that is found in them.

Meng Tse

If a man does not read with an intense desire to know the truth renouncing for its sake all that is vain and frivolous and even that which is essential if needs be, mere reading will only inspire him with pedantry, presumption and egoism.

Ramakrishna

To read too much is bad for thought. The greatest thinkers I have met among the savants whom I have studied were precisely those who were the least learned.

Lichtenberg

Having studied books, the sage uniquely consecrated to knowledge and wisdom, should leave books completely aside as a man who wants the rice abandons the husk.

Amritabindu Upanishad

We begin to know really when we succeed in forgetting completely what we have learned.

Thoreau

One arrives at such a condition only by renouncing all that one has seen, heard, understood.

Baha-ullah

So long as one has not become as simple as a child, one cannot expect the divine illumination. Forget all the knowledge of the world that you have acquired and become as ignorant as a child; then you shall attain to the divine wisdom.

Ramakrishna

The great man is he who has not lost the child's heart within him.

Meng Tse

The end of our study consists merely in recovering our heart that we have lost.

Meng Tse

The seeker who would travel in the paths of the teaching of the King of the Ancients, should purify his heart of the dark dust of human science...for it is in his heart that the divine and invisible mysteries appear transfigured.

Baha-ullah

*
**

Learn then, in brief, matter and its nature, qualities and modifications and also what the Spirit is and what its power.

Bhagavad Gita

Scrutinise the heavens, sound the earth and they will reveal to thee always their impermanence, consider the world all around thee and it will reveal to thee always its impermanence: but when thou shalt have acquired spiritual illumination, thou shalt find wisdom, and the intelligence that thou shalt have so attained will guide thee at once on the path.

Sutra in Forty-two Articles

The true royalty is spiritual knowledge; put forth thy efforts to attain it.

Farid-uddin Attar

The knowledge of the soul is the highest knowledge and truth has nothing for us beyond it.

Mahabharata

To be enlightened is to know that which is eternal.

Lao Tse

To know the One and Supreme, the supreme Lord, the immense Space, the superior Rule, that is the summit of knowledge.

Chuang Tse

When thou possessest knowledge, thou shalt attain soon to peace.

Bhagavad Gita

Which then is the cultivated and instructed soul? The one which knows the principle, end and reason diffused in all being and through all eternity and governing the whole by regular revolutions.

Marcus Aurelius

Such is the science of the Intelligence, to contemplate things divine and comprehend God.

Hermes

For those in whom self-knowledge has destroyed their ignorance, knowledge illumines sun-like that highest existence.

Bhagavad Gita

He who has plunged himself into a pure knowledge of the profoundest secrets of the Spirit, is no longer either a terrestrial or a celestial being. He is the supreme Spirit enveloped in perishable flesh, the sublime divinity itself.

Pico della Mirandola

He who suffers himself to be transported by the love of things on high, who drinks at the sources of eternal beauty, who lives by the Infinite and combats for the ideal of all virtue and all knowledge, who shows for that cult an enthusiasm pushed to a very fury — he is the hero.

Giordano Bruno

Holy Knowledge, by thee illumined, I hymn by thee the ideal light; I rejoice with the joy of the Intelligence.

Hermes

The Way of Love

Some say that knowledge is the road that leads towards love; others, that love and knowledge are interdependent.

Narada Sutra

Love is an easier method than the others; because it is self-evident and does not depend on other truths and its nature is peace and supreme felicity.

Narada Sutra

Love is greater than knowledge...because it is its own end.

Narada Sutra

Love is an invisible, a sacred and ineffable spirit which traverses the whole world with its rapid thoughts.

Empedocles

All the knowledge one can require emanates from this love.

Antoine the Healer

The knowledge of the Eternal and the love of the Eternal are in the end one and the same thing. There is no difference between pure knowledge and pure love.

Ramakrishna

Knowledge of God can be compared to a man while Love of God is like a woman. The one has his right of entry to the outer chambers of the Eternal, but only love can penetrate into the inner chambers, she who has access to the mysteries of the Almighty.

Ramakrishna

Cross even beyond the light which illumines thee and cast thyself upon the bosom of God.

Eckhart

He who goes from this world without knowing that Imperishable is poor in soul, but he who goes from this world having known that Imperishable, he is the sage.

Brihadaranyaka Upanishad

Practise with all thy strength love for that being who is the One, in order that it may be made manifest to thy sight that He is one and alone and there is no other God than He.

Ahmed Halif

Still it is not impossible to raise oneself even higher than that, for love itself is a veil between the lover and the Beloved.

Baha-ullah

The Example of the Sage

There are men in the world who labour to attain to spirituality and sages who are pure and perfect and can explain this life and the other of which they have themselves acquired the knowledge.

Book of Wisdom

There are some true and ardent aspirants who travel from place to place in search of this pass-word from a divine and perfect instructor which will open for them the doors of the eternal beatitude, and if in their earnest search one of them is so favoured as to meet such a master and receive from him the word so ardently desired which is capable of breaking all chains, he withdraws immediately from society to enter into the profound retreat of his own heart and dwells there till he has succeeded in conquering eternal peace.

Ramakrishna

The company of saints and sages is one of the chief agents of spiritual progress.

Ramakrishna

He that walketh with the wise, shall be wise.

Proverbs

For in them there is a source of intelligence, a fountain of wisdom and a flood of knowledge.

Esdras

To avoid the company of fools, to be in communion with the sages, to render honour to that which merits honour, is a great blessedness.

Mahaparinibbana Sutta

To avoid the company of fools, to take pleasure in being among the intelligent, to venerate those who are worthy of veneration, is a great blessedness.

Mahamangala Sutta

Let us lend ear to the sages who point out to us the way.

Seneca

Employ all the leisure you have in listening to the well-informed; so you shall learn without difficulty what they have learned by long labour.

Isocrates

Question attentively, then meditate at leisure over what you have heard.

Confucius

Take delight in questioning; hearken in silence to the word of the saints.

Thomas à Kempis

Happy is he who nourishes himself with these good words and shuts them up in his heart. He shall always be one of the wise.

Ecclesiasticus

He who knows how to find instructors for himself, arrives at the supreme mastery.... He who loves to ask, extends his knowledge; but whoever considers only his own personal opinion becomes constantly narrower than he was.

Shu Ching

Obey them that guide you and submit yourselves; for they watch over your souls.

Hebrews

And we beseech you to know them which labour among you and are over you and admonish you and to esteem them very highly in love for their work's sake.

I Thessalonians

Hold such in reputation.

II Philippians

Take the pearl and throw from you the shell; take the instruction which is given you by your

Master and put out of your view the human
weaknesses of the teacher.

Ramakrishna

Alone the sage can recognise the sage.

Ramakrishna

The sage increases his wisdom by all that he
can gather from others.

Fénelon

None is wise enough to guide himself alone.

Thomas à Kempis

We must choose a virtuous man to be always
present to our spirit and must live as if we were
continually under his eyes and he were scruti-
nising all that we do.

Seneca

Whosoever can cry to the All-Powerful with
sincerity and an intense passion of the soul has no

need of a Master. But so profound an aspiration is very rare; hence the necessity of a Master.

Ramakrishna

It is impossible to arrive at the summit of the mountain without passing through rough and difficult paths.

Confucius

To be ignorant of the path one has to take and set out on the way without a guide, is to will to lose onself and run the risk of perishing.

Hermes

Seek for a guide to lead you to the gates of knowledge where shines the brilliant light that is pure of all darkness.

Dhammapada

*
**

My son, if thou hearkenest to me with application thou shalt be instructed and if thou appliest thy mind thou shalt get wisdom. If thou lend thine ear, thou shalt receive instruction and if thou love to hearken thou shalt grow wise.

Ecclesiasticus

I will show thee, hear me; and that which I have seen I will declare, which wise men have told.

Job

All that man does comes to its perfection in knowledge. That do thou learn by prostration to the wise and by questioning and by serving them; they who have the knowledge and see the truths of things shall instruct thee in the knowledge.

Bhagavad Gita

Lend thine ear, hear the words of the wise, apply thy heart to knowledge.

Proverbs

Scorn not the discourse of the wise, for thou shalt learn from them wisdom.

Ecclesiasticus

Neglect not the conversation of the aged, for they speak that which they have heard from their fathers.

Ecclesiasticus

Enquire, I pray thee, of the former age and prepare thyself to search after the wisdom of their fathers.... Shall they not teach thee and tell thee words out of their heart?

Job

Avoid the society of evil friends and men of vulgar minds; have pleasure in that of the giants of wisdom and take as thy friends those who practise justice.

Dhammapada

Beyond all other men make thyself the friend of him who is distinguished by his virtue. Yield always to his gentle warnings and observe his honourable and useful actions.

Pythagoras

If thou meetest on the roads of life an intelligent friend who is following thy path, one full of justice, firmness and wisdom, then overcome all obstacles and walk at his side happy and attentive.

Dhammapada

Follow wise and intelligent men possessed of experience, patient and full of spirituality and elevation. Follow just and perfect men faithfully as the moon follows the path of the constellations.

Dhammapada

If thou remain in isolation, thou shalt never be able to travel the path of the spirit; a guide is needed. Go not alone by thyself, enter not as a blind man into that ocean.... Since thou art utterly ignorant what thou shouldst do to issue out of the pit of this world, how shalt thou dispense with a sure guide?

Farid-uddin Attar

Blush not to submit to a sage who knows more than thyself.

Democritus

Do what thy Master tells thee; it is good.

Ptah-hotep

Do not listen if one criticises or blames thy Master, leave his presence that very moment.

Ramakrishna

Hearken to the word of the sage with the ear of the soul, even when his conduct has no similitude to his teachings. Men should listen to good counsel even though it be written on a wall.

Saadi

Though my Master should visit the tavern, yet my Master shall always be a saint. Though my Master should frequent the impious meeting-place of the drunkards and the sinners, yet shall he be always to me my pure and perfect Master.

Ramakrishna

Opinions on the world and on God are many and conflicting and I know not the truth. Enlighten me, O my Master.

Hermes

Be Thy Own Torch

By three roads we can reach wisdom: the road of experience and this is the most difficult; the road of initiative and this is the easiest; and the road of reflection and this is the noblest.

Confucius

One should seek the truth himself while profiting by the directions which have reached us from ancient sages and saints.

Tolstoy

It is extravagance to ask of others what can be procured by oneself.

Seneca

The superior soul asks nothing from any but itself. The vulgar and unmeritable man asks everything of others.

Confucius

I call him a man who recognises no possessions save those he finds in himself.

Seneca

He governs his soul and expects nothing
from others.

Confucius

Be your own torch and your own refuge.
Take truth for your force, take truth for your
refuge. Seek refuge in no others but only in
yourself.

Mahaparinibbana Sutta

Who can be the Master of another? The
Eternal alone is the guide and the Master.

Ramakrishna

There are numerous Masters. But the common Master is the Universal Soul: live in it and let
its rays live in you.

Book of the Golden Precepts

It is you who must make the effort; the sages can only teach.

Dhammapada

If you do not meet a sage following the same road as yourself, then walk alone.

Dhammapada

Prepare thyself for thou must travel alone. The Master can only indicate to thee the road.

Book of the Golden Precepts

The sage is never alone;... he bears in himself the Lord of all things.

Angelus Silesius

Thou hast always a refuge in thyself.... There be free and look at all things with a fearless eye.

Marcus Aurelius

Confidence in help from outside brings with it distress. Only self-confidence gives force and joy.

Fo-shu-hing-tsan-king

Stimulate thyself, direct thyself; thus protected by thyself and full of clear-seeing thou shalt live always happy.

Dhammapada

Shine out for thyself as thy own light.

Dhammapada

Be thy own torch; rise up and become wise.

Book of Wisdom

Intellectual Independence

Do not believe all that men say.

Ecclesiasticus

Leave out of your mind the quality of him who speaks to you whether great or small, and consider with an open mind whether the words spoken are true or false.

Iamblichus

Do not believe in men's discourses before you have reflected well on them.

Shu Ching

Do not believe a thing simply upon hearsay. Do not believe on the authority of traditions merely because they have been held in honour by numerous generations. Do not believe a thing because the general opinion holds it for the truth and because men speak much of it. Do not believe a thing because one of the wise men of antiquity bears witness to it. Do not believe a thing because the probabilities are in its favour, or because long habit has accustomed you to think of it as the truth. Do not believe in things you have imagined, thinking that a superior Power has revealed them to you. Do not believe anything upon the sole authority of your masters or of priests.

What you have tried and experienced yourself and recognised as the Truth, what is in conformity with your own good and the good of others, in that believe and order your conduct accordingly.

Anguttara Nikaya

Beloved, believe not every spirit... because many false prophets are gone out into the world.

John

Even if the whole world should believe in the truth of a doctrine and if it should be very ancient, man ought to control it by his reason and throw it boldly away if it does not agree with the demands of his reason.

Tolstoy

The more people believe in one thing, the more one ought to be careful with regard to that belief and attentive in examining it.

Tolstoy

Let not the talk of the vulgar make any impression on you.

Cicero

Nothing is so dangerous as the habit we have of referring to a common opinion. So long as one trusts other people without taking the trouble to judge for oneself, one lives by the faith of others, error is passed on from hand to hand and example destroys us.

Seneca

To believe blindly is bad. Reason, judge for yourselves, experiment, verify whether what you have been told is true or false.

Vivekananda

Use your body and your thought and turn away from anybody who asks you to believe blindly, whatever be his good will or his virtue.

Vivekananda

Be not children in understanding, be men.

I Corinthians

Prove all things; hold fast that which is good.

I Thessalonians

Put all things to the touchstone of your reason, to a free and independent scrutiny and keep what is good, what is true, what is useful.

Huxley

If you wish to battle and strive for Truth become a thinker, that is to say, a free man.

Apollonius of Tyana

Be then on your guard against everything that suppresses your liberty.

Vivekananda

The wise man should not act under constraint but remain free in his actions.

Democritus

Attentive in the midst of the heedless, awake amidst sleepers, the intelligent man walks on leaving the others as far behind him as a courser distances beasts of burden.

Dhammapada

Moral Independence

Often man is preoccupied with human rules and forgets the inner law.

Antoine the Healer

The superior type of man is in all the circumstances of his life exempt from prejudices and obstinacy; he regulates himself by justice alone.

Confucius

The just man is himself his own law.

Catacombs Inscription

It is better to follow one's own law even though imperfect than the better law of another.

Bhagavad Gita

A soul full of wisdom, however excellent it be, cannot be compared with right and straightforward Thought.

Fo-shu-hing-tsan-king

A man's heart showeth to him what he should do better than seven sentinels on the summit of a rock.

Ecclesiasticus

Often men take for their conscience not the manifestation of the spiritual being but simply what is considered good or bad by the people in their environment.

Tolstoy

What human voice is capable of telling me, "This is good and that is bad?"

Kobo Daishi

Do what thou knowest to be good without expecting from it any glory. Forget not that the vulgar are a bad judge of good actions.

Demophilus

It is better to be good and to be called wicked by men than to be wicked and esteemed good.

Saadi

Whoever wishes to be truly a man, must abandon all preoccupation by the wish to please the world. There is nothing more sacred or more fecund than the curiosity of an independent spirit.

Emerson

Only one who has surmounted by wisdom that which the world calls good and evil and who lives in a clear light, can be truly called an ascetic.

Dhammapada

When you raise yourself beyond praise and blame and your will, the will of a man who loves, intends to be master of all things, then for you is the beginning of virtue.

Nietzsche

But the higher you raise yourself, the smaller you will seem to the eyes that are envious. He who ranges on the heights is the one whom men most detest.

Nietzsche

If a man is detested by the crowd, you must examine, before you judge him, why they condemn, and if a man is venerated by the crowd, equally must you, before you judge, examine why they admire.

Confucius

Let us take care above all not to walk like a flock of sheep each in the other's traces; let us inform ourselves rather of the place where we ought to go than of that where others are going.

Seneca

They will renounce even the treading in the tracks of their fathers and ancestors. They will shut the doors of friendship and hatred on all the dwellers in the world.

Baha-ullah

Break, break the old Tables, ye who seek after the knowledge.

Nietzsche

Neither do men put new wine into old bottles.

Matthew

I love the great scorners because they are the great worshippers, arrows shot by desire towards that other shore.

Nietzsche

To Know the Impermanence of Things

Things mortal change their aspect daily; they are nothing but a lie.

Hermes

The disciple should think that all things in this world are subject to a constant transformation,... that all things in the past are like a dream, that all in the present are like a flash of lightning and all in the future like images that arrive spontaneously into existence.

Ashwaghosha

Matter is like a stream in perpetual flow; the actions of Nature manifest by continual mutations and endless transformations. There is hardly anything that is stable. Behold near thee this immense abyss of the times that no longer are and the future in which all things will disappear.

Marcus Aurelius

All is movement and nothing is fixed; we cannot cross over the same stream twice.

Heraclitus

Everything that is composite is soon destroyed and, like the lightning in heaven, does not last for long.

Lalita Vistara

What desolates my heart, is this sort of continual destruction throughout Nature; she has created nothing which does not destroy its neighbour or destroy itself. Thus, staggering and bewildered in the midst of these oscillating forces of earth and heaven, I move forward seeing nothing but a world in which all devours and ruminates eternally.

Goethe

It is a horrible thing to feel continually passing away everything which one possesses or to which one can attach oneself and yet to have no desire to seek out whether there is not something permanent.

Pascal

Therefore seek one thing only, — the kingdom of the permanent.

Book of Wisdom

The contemplation of impermanence is a door which leads to liberation and dissolves the formations of Illusion.

Abhidhammattha Sangaha

If one ponders well, one finds that all that passes has never truly existed.

Schopenhauer

With the comprehension of the nature, impermanent, void of reality in itself and subject to grief, of all things, the sun of the true wisdom rises. Without this comprehension there can be no real light.

Fo-shu-hing-tsan-king

All aggregations are transient, all aggregations are subject to sorrow, all aggregations are without any substantial reality; when one is entirely penetrated with this fact, one is delivered from sorrow. This is the way of purification.

Dhammapada

When thou hast recognised the impermanence of all formations, thou shalt contemplate that which does not perish and remains forever.

Book of Wisdom

The external forms are alone subject to change and destruction; for these forms are not the things themselves.

Giordano Bruno

Deliver thyself from the inconstancy of human things.

Seneca

To Understand the Unreality of the Ego

Life is a journey in the darkness of the night.

Panchatantra

What is human life? A bubble on a torrent produced by the rain, which dances and balances itself gaily on the waves, full of new life. And suddenly it bursts and disappears leaving no trace to mark hereafter the place that for a few moments it had occupied.

Zeisho Aisuko

Dewdrops fall on the large leaves of a lotus, they remain there trembling for a brief moment and then glide one this way and one another way and disappear. Such is life.

Sojo Henjo

Life is no more than a drop of water which shines upon a flower and even as it sparkles, glides away and disappears, and all our actions are no more than clouds reflected in a dewdrop; they are dreams that pass and disappear with the dreamer.

Tyotomi Hideyoshi

If we dreamed every night the same thing, it would affect us as much as the objects which we see every day.

Pascal

The world is a dream and resembles a flower in bloom which shakes out to all its sides its pollen and then no longer is.

Minamoto Sanetomo

The world is but a dream that passes and neither happiness nor sorrow are enduring.

Firdausi

And in this world, always a work of Illusion, men whose intelligence is troubled by desire, greed, envy and error, are rolled through different states with the idea that these states are real.

Bhagavata Purana

Men direct their gaze upon fugitive appearances and the transitory brilliance of this world of the senses and they lend no attention to the immutable Reality which remains unknown to them.

Takeda Shingen

*
**

Thou hast demanded of me what is this phantasmagoria of things here around us. To tell thee the whole truth of this matter would take too long; it is a fantastic image which issues from a vast ocean and then into that vast ocean it returns.

Omar Khayyam

The tranquil lake reflects in the polished mirror of its waters heaven and the trees and the glittering stars; approach now and see how the image is changed; in place of heaven and the stars it is thyself that thou seest, for it was thy soul that created the heaven and the stars reflected in the mirror of the lake. Learn that all things seem to be in the soul which reflects them, but they are not the truth and the essence of the eternal reality. That essence is in the Spirit which forms all things.

Anonymous

Everything is but a shadow cast by the mind.

Ashwaghosha

All things, simply by reason of our confused subjectivity, appear in the forms of individuali-sation. If we could raise ourselves above our confused subjectivity, the signs of individuality would disappear and there would be no trace of a world of objects.

Ashwaghosha

We can thus recognise that all phenomena of the world are only the illusory manifestations of the mind and have no reality proper to themselves.

Ashwaghosha

Thus Space exists only in relation to our particularising consciousness.

Ashwaghosha

Space is only a mode of particularisation and has no real self-existence.

Ashwaghosha

All the modes of relative existence of our phenomenal world are simply created by particularisation in the troubled mind.

Ashwaghosha

Although all things in their metaphysical origin proceed from the soul one and truly free from all particularisation, nevertheless by reason of non-illumination there is produced a subjective mind which becomes conscious of an external world.

Ashwaghosha

The senses and the mind seek to convince thee, so vain are they, that they are the end of all things. The senses and the mind are only instruments and playthings. Behind the feelings and the thoughts, my brother, there dwells a more puissant master, an unknown sage; it is called the Self.

Nietzsche

It is on the blindness of ignorance that is founded the working which affirms the ego.

Sanyutta Nikaya

How vain and unreal, when I reflect, becomes this ego which I call mine! Yet a little time and behold! it is dispersed to all the winds and dissolution has effaced it.

Mikado Shujaku

The egoist sacrifices everything to his "I", dupe of an error which makes him take his personality for something real and durable and the world of phenomena for a solid entity. Thus life

under this form of unbridled individualism is void
of all moral character.

Schopenhauer

The thought of the ego occupies only the
man of unsound understanding, the sage recognises that it has no foundation; he examines the
world rationally and concludes that all formations
of existence are vain and hasten towards dissolution; alone the Law remains eternal. When man
by his efforts has acquired this knowledge he
contemplates the truth.

Fo-shu-hing-tsan-king

It is thus that by the study of principles is
produced this science which consists in saying, "I
am not that; this is not mine; this is not myself" —
a science definitive, pure from all kind of doubt, a
science absolute and unique.

Sankhya Karika

The body, the sensations, the perception, the

respective differentiations and the mental consciousness are not the self.

Book of Wisdom

The body is the name of a succession of changes; it is with the body as with a river in which you see the same form, but the waves change every moment and other and new waves take the place of those that preceded them.

Vivekananda

The body is like a bubbling on the surface of water; sensation is like its foam; perception resembles a mirage; consciousness is like a hallucination.

Book of Wisdom

Regard incessantly this body as the bespangled chariot of a king; it gladdens the simpleton but not the wise, dazzles the fool but not the sage.

Udanavagga

Rely on nothing that thy senses perceive; all that thou seest, hearest, feelest is like a deceiving dream.

Minamoto Sanetomo

Terrestrial things are not the truth, but semblances of truth.

Hermes

To Renounce the Illusion
of the World

A mind without wisdom remains the sport of illusion and miserable.

Fo-shu-hing-tsan-king

Men insensate enter into the world seduced by a false brilliance. But just as it is easier to enter into a net than to issue out of it, so is it easier to enter into the world than to renounce it when once one has entered in.

Ramakrishna

That man whose mind is solely attached to the objects of sense, him death drags with it as an impetuous torrent sweeps away a slumbering village.

Dhammapada

The foolish follow after outward desires and they enter into the snare of death that is wide-extended for them; but the wise, having found immortality, know that which is sure and desire not here uncertain things.

Katha Upanishad

The wise do not linger in the thicket of the senses, the wise heed not the honeyed voices of the illusion.

Book of Golden Precepts

So long as we are attached to the form, we shall be unable to appreciate the substance, we shall have no notion of the causes the knowledge of which is the true knowing.

Antoine the Healer

Before the soul can see, it must have acquired the inner harmony and made the eyes blind to all illusion.

Book of Golden Precepts

He whose senses are not attached to name

and form, who is no longer troubled by transient things, can be really called a disciple.

Dhammapada

He who discerns the truth as truth and the illusion as an illusion, attains to the truth and is walking in the right road.

Dhammapada

If you wish to know why we must renounce all semblances, the reason is this that they are only means to lead us to the simple and naked truth. If I wish, then, to arrive at that truth I must leave behind me little by little the road which leads me to it.

Tauler

The knowledge of the divine nature is the sole truth and this truth cannot be discovered, nor even its shadow, in this world full of lies, of changing appearances and of errors.

Hermes

As clouds cover the sun, so the Illusion hides the Divinity. When the clouds recede, the sun becomes visible; even so when the Illusion is dissipated, the Eternal can be seen.

Ramakrishna

You veil your eyes and complain that you cannot see the Eternal. If you wish to see Him, tear from your eyes the veil of the illusion.

Ramakrishna

So and likewise, if you tear away the veils of the heart, the light of the oneness will shine upon it.

Baha-ullah

O disciple, that which was not created dwells in thee. If thou wish to attain to it...thou must strip thyself of thy dark robes of illusion.

Book of Golden Precepts

Flee the Ignorance and flee also the Illusion.

Turn thy face from the deceptions of the world;
distrust thy senses, they are liars. But in thy body
which is the tabernacle of sensation, seek the
"Eternal Man".

Book of Golden Precepts

The world is a brilliant flame in which every
moment a new creature comes to burn itself.
Bravely turn thy eyes from it like the lion, if thou
wouldst not burn thyself in it like the butterfly. The
insensate who like that insect adores the flame,
will surely be burned in it.

Farid-uddin Attar

This is the new birth, my son, to turn one's
thought from the body that has the three dimen-
sions.

Hermes

What then is that which is true? That which
is not troubled, my son, that which has no limits,
colour nor form, the unmoving, the naked, the

luminous, that which knows itself, the immutable, the good, the incorporeal.

Hermes

In what then consists progress? He who detaching himself from external things devotes himself entirely to the education and preparation of his faculty of judgment and will in order to put it into accord with Nature and give it elevation, freedom, independence, self-possession — he it is who is really progressing.

Epictetus

Who truly travels beyond the Illusion? He who renounces evil associations, who keeps company with lofty spirits, who has no longer the sense of possession; who frequents solitary places; who wrests himself out of slavery to the world, passes beyond the three qualities and abandons all anxiety about his existence; renounces the fruits of works, renounces his works and becomes free from the opposites; who renounces even the Vedas and aids others to travel beyond; he truly travels beyond and helps others to make the voyage.

Narada Sutra

He who has surmounted the furious waves of visible things, of him it is said, "He is a master of the wisdom." He has attained the bank, he stands on firm ground. If thou hast traversed this sea with its abysms, full of waves, full of depths, full of monsters, then wisdom and holiness are thy portion. Thou hast attained to land, thou hast attained to the aim of the universe.

Sanyutta Nikaya

He alone traverses the current of the illusion who comes face to face with the Eternal and realises it.

Ramakrishna

I will therefore make ready to render my thought an alien to the illusion of the world.

Hermes

Look Within Things

Look within things.

Marcus Aurelius

Let us attach ourselves to a solid good, to a good that shines within and not externally. Let us devote all our efforts to its discovery.

Seneca

Attach thyself to the sense of things and not to their form. The sense is the essential, the form is only an encumbrance.

Farid-uddin Attar

Seeing many things, yet thou observest not; opening the ears ye hear not.

Isaiah

Eye and ear are poor witnesses for man, if his inner life has not been made fine.

Heraclitus

Thence comes it that the saint occupies himself with his inner being and not with the objects of his eyes.

Lao Tse

How canst thou seize by the senses that which is neither solid nor liquid,... that which is conceived only in power and energy?

Hermes

Empty for the fool are all the points of space.

Hindu Saying

So long as the mind stops at the observation of multiple details, it does not enter into the general field of true knowledge.

Patanjali

When the mind has been trained on its object, it transforms itself to the image of that which it scrutinises and enters into the full comprehension of what it finds therein contained.

Patanjali

There is nothing, however small, however vile it be, that does not contain mind.

Giordano Bruno

In each thing there is a door to knowledge and in each atom is seen the trace of the sun.

Baha-ullah

In the interior of each atom that thou shalt cleave, thou shalt find imprisoned a sun.

Ahmed Halif

In each atom thou shalt see the All, thou shalt contemplate millions of secrets as luminous as the sun.

Farid-uddin Attar

When one discovers the enigma of a single atom, one can see the mystery of all creation, that within us as well as that without.

Mohyuddin ibn Arabi

In this immense ocean the world is an atom and the atom a world.

Farid-uddin Attar

If thou understand, what seems invisible to most shall be to thee very apparent.

Hermes

If we raise ourselves for a moment by aesthetic contemplation above the heavy terrestrial atmosphere, we are then beings blessed over all.

Schopenhauer

That is why the incorporeal eye should be raised to contemplate not the figure, not the body, not the appearance, but that which is calm, tranquil, solid, immutable.

Hermes

We look not at the things which are seen, but at the things which are not seen; for the things which are seen are temporal, but the things which are not seen are eternal.

II Corinthians

There is a natural body and there is a spiritual body.

I Corinthians

There is a supreme state unmanifest beyond this Nature and eternal which perishes not when all creatures perish; it is unmanifest and immutable and the supreme goal.

Bhagavad Gita

Three worlds: the world of desire, the world of form and the world of the formless.

Sanyutta Nikaya

Yes, my brother, if we think of each world, we shall find there a hundred thousand wonderful sciences. One of these worlds is Sleep. What problems it contains! what wisdom is there concealed! how many worlds it includes!

Baha-ullah

For the waking there is only one common world.... During sleep each turns towards his own particular world.

Heraclitus

My heart within instructs me also in the night seasons.

Psalms

The Mastery of the Mind

They had attained to the supreme perfection
of being completely masters of their thought.

The Lotus of Bliss

Be master of thy thoughts, O thou who
wrestlest for perfection.

Book of Golden Precepts

Be master of thy soul, O seeker of the eternal
truths, if thou wouldst attain the goal.

Book of Golden Precepts

The soul not being mistress of itself, one
looks but sees not, listens but hears not.

Tseng Tse

The self is master of the self; what other
master can it have? The sage who has made

himself master of himself, rends his bonds and breaks his chains.

Udanavagga

The self is master of itself, what other master can it have? A self well-controlled is a master difficult to procure.

Dhammapada

To be master of one's mind! how difficult that is! it has been compared, not without reason, to a mad monkey.

Vivekananda

The mind is difficult to restrain, light, running whither it pleases; to control it is a helpful thing; controlled, it secures happiness.

Dhammapada

The mind is restless, violent, powerful, obstinate; its control seems to me as difficult a task as to control the wind.

Bhagavad Gita

Just as the fly settles now on an unclean sore and now on the sweetmeats offered to the gods, so a worldly man's thoughts stop for a moment on religious subjects and the next stray into the pleasures of luxury and lust.

Ramakrishna

So long as the mentality is inconstant and inconsequent, it is worthless, though one have a good teacher and the company of holy men.

Ramakrishna

On his mind vacillating, mobile, difficult to hold in, difficult to master, the intelligent man should impose the same straightness as an arrow-maker gives to an arrow.

Dhammapada

Abandoning without exception all desires born of the will, controlling by the mind the senses in all directions, a man should gradually cease from mental action by the force of an understanding held in the grasp of a constant will; he should fix his mind in the self and think of nothing at all, and whenever the restless and mobile mentality ranges forth he should draw it back from whatever direction it takes and bring it again under control in the self alone: for when the mind has thus been quieted, there comes to man the highest peace.

Bhagavad Gita

The wise man should rein in intently this mental action like a chariot drawn by untrained horses.

Shwetashwatara Upanishad

A half-attention prepares the way for fresh errors, fresh illusions and allows the old to increase. Prevent by a sustained attention the birth of new errors and destroy the old.

Majjhima Nikaya

Under all circumstances be vigilant.

Baha-ullah

Let us watch over our thoughts.

Fo-shu-hing-tsan-king

A bad thought is the most dangerous of thieves.

Chinese Buddhist Scriptures

Let not worldly thoughts and anxieties trouble your minds.

Ramakrishna

Have no vicious thoughts.

Confucius

When a thought rises in us, let us see whether it is not in touch with the inferior worlds.

Antoine the Healer

When the disciple considering an idea sees rise in him bad or unhealthy thoughts, thoughts of covetousness, hatred or error, he should either turn his mind away from that idea or concentrate it upon a healthy thought, or else examine the fatal nature of the idea, or analyse it and decompose it into its different elements, or, making appeal to all his strength and applying the greatest energy, suppress it from his mind; thus are removed and disappear these bad and unhealthy ideas and the mind becomes firm, calm, unified, full of vigour.

Ashwaghosha

By dominating the senses one increases the intelligence.

Mahabharata

*
**

The mind is a clear and polished mirror and our continual duty is to keep it pure and never allow dust to accumulate upon it.

Hindu Saying

When a mirror is covered with dust it cannot reflect images; it can only do so when it is clear of stain. So is it with beings. If their minds are not pure of soil, the Absolute cannot reveal itself in them. But if they free themselves from soil, then of itself it will be revealed.

Ashwaghosha

Action like inaction may find its place in thee; if thy body is in movement, let thy mind be calm, let thy soul be as limpid as a mountain lake.

Book of Golden Precepts

When water is still, it reflects objects like a mirror. This stillness, this perfect level is the model of the sage. If water is translucent when it is in perfect rest, much more so must it be with the intellectual essence. The heart of the sage in perfect repose is the mirror of earth and heaven and all existences.

Chuang Tse

Even as the troubled surface of rolling waters cannot properly reflect the full moon, but only gives broken images of it, so a mind troubled by the desires and passions of the world cannot fully reflect the light of the Ineffable.

Ramakrishna

The Eternal is seen when the mind is at rest. When the sea of the mind is troubled by the winds of desire, it cannot reflect the Eternal and all divine vision is impossible.

Ramakrishna

Concentration

The power of the human intelligence is without bounds; it increases by concentration: that is the secret.

Vivekananda

The force of attention properly guided and directed towards the inner life allows us to analyse our soul and will shed light on many things. The forces of the mind resemble scattered rays; concentrate them and they illumine everything. That is the sole source of knowledge we possess; to conquer this knowledge there is only one method, concentration.

Vivekananda

Just as the penetrating rays of the sun visit the darkest corners, so thought concentrated will master its own deepest secrets.

Vivekananda

Once the mind has been trained to fix itself on formed images, it can easily accustom itself to fix on formless realities.

Ramakrishna

So we should acquire the power of concentration by fixing the mind first on forms and when we have obtained in this a full success, we can easily fix it on the formless.

Ramakrishna

The powers developed are liable to become obstacles to a perfect concentration by reason of the possibility of wonder and admiration which results from their exercise.

Patanjali

The obstacles met by the seeker after concentration are illness, langour, doubt, negligence, idleness, the domination of the senses, false perception, impotence to attain and instability in a state of meditation once attained.

Patanjali

Such difficulties are root and product of both physical and mental workings; they produce their fruits alike in the visible and invisible.

Patanjali

When we render natural and easy to us perfect concentration (or the operation which consists in fixing attention, contemplation and meditation), a power of exact discernment develops.

Patanjali

After long practice one who is master of himself can dispense with diverse aids to concentration...and he will be able to make himself master of any result whatsoever simply by desiring it.

Patanjali

When by a constant practice a man is capable of effecting mental concentration, then wherever he may be, his mind will always lift itself above his surroundings and will repose in the Eternal.

Ramakrishna

The greater his aspiration and concentration, the more he finds the Eternal.

Ramakrishna

Contemplation

Whoever applies himself intelligently to profound meditation, soon finds joy in what is good; he becomes conscious that beauty and riches are transient things and wisdom the fairest ornament.

Fo-shu-hing-tsan-king

He thinks actively, he opens his heart, he gathers up his internal illuminations.

Lao Tse

How can he be long in peace who troubles himself with foreign cares, who seeks to diffuse himself into the outward and withdraws little or rarely into himself?

Thomas à Kempis

Without contemplation there is no tranquillity and without tranquillity how shall there be happiness? The mind that orders itself according to the motions of the senses, carries away the intelligence as the wind carries away a ship on the sea. Therefore only he whose senses are drawn back from the objects of sense, has a firmly seated wisdom.

Bhagavad Gita

Let him destroy by deep meditation the qualities that are opposed to the divine nature.

Laws of Manu

As in a house with a sound roof the rain cannot penetrate, so in a mind where meditation dwells passion cannot enter.

Dhammapada

Having attained to that unalterable calm which nothing can trouble, one can afterwards meditate and form an assured judgment on the essence of things; when one has meditated and formed a sure judgment on the essence of things, afterwards one can attain to the desired state of perfection.

Confucius

One who during his contemplation is entirely inconscient of all external things to such a point that if birds made a nest in his hair he would not know it, has acquired the perfection of meditation.

Ramakrishna

He will go from doubt to certitude, from the night of error to the light of the Guidance; he will see with the eye of knowledge and begin to converse in secret with the Well-beloved.

Baha-ullah

"To him who is perfect in meditation salvation is near" is an old saying. Do you know when a man is perfect in meditation? When as soon as he sits to meditate, he is surrounded with the divine atmosphere and his soul communes with the Ineffable.

Ramakrishna

Meditate on the Eternal either in an unknown nook or in the solitude of the forests or in the solitude of thy own mind.

Ramakrishna

Silence thy thoughts and fix all thy attention on the Master within whom thou seest not yet, but of whom thou hast a presentiment.

Book of Golden Precepts

His form stands not within the vision of any, none seeth Him with the eye. By the heart and the thought and the mind He is experienced; who seize this with the knowledge, they become immortal.

Katha Upanishad

He is not seized by the eye, nor by the speech, nor by the other gods, nor by the austerity of force, nor by action; when a man's being has been purified by a calm clarity of knowledge, he meditating beholds that which has not parts nor members.

Mundaka Upanishad

One who has not ceased from evil living or is without peace or without concentration or whose mind has not been tranquillised, cannot attain to Him by the intelligence.

Katha Upanishad

This self can always be won by truth and austerity, by purity and by entire knowledge.

Mundaka Upanishad

When thy understanding shall stand immovable and unshakable in concentration, then thou shalt attain to the divine Union.

Bhagavad Gita

Those who pursue attentively their contemplation have no sorrow to fear, nor can any vicissitude of Fate affect them. They contemplate this history written in ourselves to guide us in the execution of the divine laws which, equally, are engraved in our hearts.

Giordano Bruno

Silence

And, first, ordinarily be silent.

Epictetus

For the ignorant there is no better rule than silence and if he knew its advantage he would not be ignorant.

Saadi

The seeker ought to avoid any preference of himself to another; he should efface pride and arrogance from his heart, arm himself with patience and endurance and follow the law of silence so that he may keep himself from vain words.

Baha-ullah

My brothers, when you accost each other, two things alone are fitting, instructive words or a grave silence.

Buddhist Scripture

It is far more useful to commune with oneself than with others.

Demophilus

The word echoes more profoundly in thyself than from the mouth of others. If thou canst listen for it in silence, thou shalt hear it at once.

Angelus Silesius

Before the soul can understand and remember it must be united to Him who speaks by His silence, as to the mind of the potter the form on which the clay is modelled.

Book of Golden Precepts

The eyes of our mentality are incapable as yet of contemplating the incorruptible and incomprehensible Beauty.... Thou shalt see it when thou hast nothing to say concerning it; for knowledge, for contemplation are silence, are the sinking to rest of all sensation.

Hermes

So long as a man cries aloud, O Allah, O Allah, be sure he has not yet found his Allah; for whoever has found Him becomes calm and full of peace.

Ramakrishna

It is God within who hushes the tongue of prayer by a sublimer thought. A voice speaks to us in the depths of the heart, "I am, my child, and by me are and subsist thy body and the luminous world. I am: all things are in me and all that is mine is thine."

Emerson

When one considers the clamorous emptiness of the world, words of so little sense, actions of so little merit, one loves to reflect on the great reign of silence. The noble silent men scattered here and there each in his province silently thinking and silently acting of whom no morning paper makes mention, these are the salt of the earth.

Carlyle

Real action is done in moments of silence.

Emerson

The ancients might well make of silence a god, for it is the element of all divinity, of all infinity, of all transcendent greatness, at once the source and the ocean in which all begins and ends.

Carlyle

Silence, the great empire of silence, loftier than the stars, profounder than the kingdom of Death! It alone is great; all the rest is petty.

Carlyle

SECTION II

THE PRACTICE OF TRUTH

To Practise

If you live one sixth of what is taught you, you will surely attain the goal.

Ramakrishna

Since the important thing is to practise, it is in vain that one is near the master if one does not practise oneself; no profit of any kind comes out of it.

Sutra in Forty-two Articles

The mind may be compared to a precious stone which is pure and brilliant in itself but hidden in a coarse coating of foulness. There is no reason to suppose that anyone will be able to clean and purify it simply by gazing at it without any process of cleansing.

Ashwaghosha

It is not difficult to know the good, but it is difficult to put it in practice.

Shu Ching

The man who knows the principles of right reason is less than the man who loves them, and he less than the man who makes of them his delight and practises them.

Confucius

Better are those who read than those who have studied little; preferable those who possess what they have read to those who have read and forgotten; more meritorious those who understand than those who know by heart; those to be more highly valued who do their duty than those who merely know it.

Laws of Manu

Hindu almanacs contain predictions about the annual rains foretelling how many centimetres will fall in the country; but by pressing the book which is so full of predictions of rain, you will extract not a drop of water. So also many good words are to be found in pious books, but the mere reading of them does not give spirituality.

Ramakrishna

There are two persons who have given themselves useless trouble and made efforts without profit. One is he who has amassed wealth and has spent it and the other is he who has acquired knowledge and has made no use of it.

Saadi

The man of knowledge without a good heart is like the bee without honey.

Saadi

The knowledge one does not practise is a poison.

Hitopadesha

Intelligence divorced from virtue is no longer intelligence.

Minokhired

All good thoughts, good words, good actions are works of intelligence; all bad thoughts, bad words, bad actions are words of unintelligence.

Zend-Avesta

Freedom from pride and arrogance, harmlessness, patience, sincerity, purity, constancy, self-control, indifference to the objects of sense, absence of egoism, ... freedom from attachment to son and wife and house, constant equality of heart towards desirable or undesirable events, love of solitude and withdrawal from the crowd, perpetual knowledge of the Supreme and study of the principle of things, this is knowledge; what is contrary in nature to this, is ignorance.

Bhagavad Gita

One may say boldly that no man has a just perception of any truth, if that truth has not reacted on him so intensely that he is ready to be its martyr.

Emerson

Speak well, act better.

Catinat

Apply thyself to think what is good, speak what is good, do what is good.

Zend-Avesta

Let your words correspond with your actions and your actions with your words.

Confucius

Act as you speak.

Lalita Vistara

As the perfect man speaks so he acts; as he acts, so the perfect man speaks. It is because he speaks as he acts and acts as he speaks that he is called the perfect.

Buddhist Scripture

Who is the superior man? It is he who first

puts his words in practice and then speaks in agreement with his acts.

Confucius

Ordinary men pronounce a sackful of discourses on religion, but do not put a grain into practice, while the sage speaks little, but his whole life is religion put into action.

Ramakrishna

Fine language not followed by acts in harmony with it is like a splendid flower brilliant in colour but without perfume.

Dhammapada

To conform one's conduct to one's talk is an eminent virtue; attain to that virtue and then you may speak of the duties of others.

Li Chi

Thou wouldst exhort men to good? but hast thou exhorted thyself? Thou wouldst be useful to them? Show by thy own example what men philosophy can make and do not prate uselessly.

Epictetus

Improve others not by reasoning but by example. Let your existence, not your words, be your preaching.

Amiel

Make yourself loved by the example of your life.

St. Vincent de Paul

Bad example is a spiritual poisoning of men.

Amiel

*
**

The tree is known by its fruits.

Matthew

Gold is tested by the fire, the good man by

his acts, heroes by perils, the prudent man by difficult circumstances, friends and enemies by great needs.

Mahabharata

Virtue shows itself in the lowest as well as in the sublimest things.

Confucius

Now that you have learned to know the truth, let your hearts henceforth enlightened take pleasure in a conduct in conformity with it.

Fo-shu-hing-tsan-king

The True Cult:
The Religion of the Spirit

If you have art and science, you have religion;
if you have neither art nor science, then have
religion.

Goethe

Why do you amass stones and construct
great temples?

Why do you vex yourselves thus when God
dwells within you?

Vemana

Temples cannot imprison within their walls
the divine Substance.

Euripides

The soul of each man contains the potential
divinity. Our aim must be to make apparent this
divinity within us by subduing our inner and outer
nature. Attain to him by works or by adoration, by

physical mastery, by philosophy, by one, by several or by all of these methods and be free. That is the whole of religion. Doctrines, dogmas, rituals, books, temples, forms are only secondary details.

Vivekananda

Although there is a difference of procedure between a Shaman of the Tungas and a Catholic prelate of Europe or between a coarse and sensual Vogul and a Puritan Independent of Connecticut, there is no difference in the principle of their creeds; for they all belong to the same category of people whose religion consists not in becoming better, but in believing in the carrying out of certain arbitrary regulations. Only those who believe that the worship of God consists in aspiring to a better life differ from the first because they recognise quite another and certainly a loftier principle uniting all men of good faith in an invisible temple which alone can be the universal temple.

Kant

Everywhere something hinders me from meeting God in my brother because he has shut the doors of his inmost temple and recites the fables of his brother's god or the god of his brother's brother.

Emerson

How astonishing is this that of all the supreme revelations of the truth the world admits and tolerates only the more ancient, those which answer least to the needs of our epoch, while it holds each direct revelation, each original thought for null and sometimes hates them.

Thoreau

One should not think that a religion is true because it is old. On the contrary the more mankind lives, the more the true law of life becomes clear to it. To suppose that in our epoch one must continue to believe what grandfathers and ancestors believed is to think that an adult can continue to wear the garments of children.

Tseng Tse

That is why the superior man or he who is identified with the straight path watches attentively in his heart for the principles which have not been discerned by all and meditates with care on that which is not yet proclaimed and recognised as doctrine.

Chung Yung

Note this well that from whencesoever it may come, a teaching which leads to passion and not to peace, to pride and not to modesty, to the extension of desire and not to its moderation, to the love of worldliness and not to the love of solitude, to a violent and not to a peaceful spirit, is not the Law, is not the Discipline, is not the teaching of the Master.

Vinaya Pitaka

The Church does not consist in a great number of persons. He who possesses the Truth at his side is the Church, though he be alone.

Ibn Masud

Let us not fear to reject from our religion all that is useless, material, tangible as well as all that is vague and indefinite; the more we purify its spiritual kernel, the more we shall understand the true law of life.

Tolstoy

It is useless to grow pale over the holy Scriptures and the sacred Shastras without a spirit of discrimination exempt from all passions. No spiritual progress can be made without discrimination and renunciation.

Ramakrishna

For the letter killeth, but the spirit giveth life.

II Corinthians

Beware of the scribes who desire to walk in long robes and love greetings in the markets and the highest seats in the synagogues and the chief places at feasts, who devour widows' houses and for a show make long prayers.

Luke

And there are others who wallow in their bogs and squatting among the rushes set themselves to cry, "This is virtue, to remain quiet in a bog." Their knees are ever bent and their hands joined in praise of virtue, but their hearts know it not.

Nietzsche

Men never commit bad actions with more coolness and assurance in their rectitude than when they do them by virtue of a false belief.

Pascal

Visit not the doers of miracles. They have wandered from the path of the truth; they have allowed their minds to be caught in the snare of psychical powers which are so many temptations on the path of the pilgrims to the Brahman. Beware of such powers and do not desire them.

Ramakrishna

He whose heart longs after the Deity, has no time for anything else.

Ramakrishna

He is a stranger to the magical arts and divination and necromancy, to exorcisms and other analogous practices. He takes no part in the accomplishment of any prayer or religious ceremony.

Digha Nikaya

He whose thought is always fixed on the Eternal has no need of any devotional practice or spiritual exercise.

Ramakrishna

After having abandoned every kind of pious practice, directing his mind towards the sole object of his thoughts, the contemplation of the divine Being, free from all desire...he attains the supreme goal.

Laws of Manu

The Religion of Love

Render to God the sole worship which is fitting towards Him: not to be evil.

Hermes

True worship does not consist in offering incense, flowers and other material objects, but in striving to follow the same path as the object of our veneration.

Jatakamala

Not superstitious rites but self-control allied to benevolence and beneficence towards all beings are in truth the rites one should accomplish in all places.

Ashoka

Speak the truth, do not abandon yourself to wrath, give of the little you have to those who seek your aid. By these three steps you shall approach the Gods.

Dhammapada

It is much better to observe justice than to pass one's whole life in the prostrations and genuflexions of an external worship.

Farid-uddin Attar

Though a man should have lived a hundred years consecrating his whole life to the performance of numerous sacrifices to the gods, all this is far from having the same worth as a single act of love which consists in succouring a life.

Fa-ken-pi-u

A hundred years of life passed without the vision of the supreme law are not worth a single day of a life consecrated to that vision.

Dhammapada

What is the path that leads to the Eternal? When a disciple pours over the whole world the light of a heart overflowing with love, in all directions, on high, below, to the four quarters, with a thought of love, large, profound, boundless, void of wrath and hate, and when thereafter he pours over the whole world the light of a thought of profound serenity, then the disciple is on the path that leads to the Eternal.

Anguttara Nikaya

*
**

In what does religion consist? It consists in causing as little suffering as possible and in doing good in abundance. It consists in the practice of love, of compassion, of truth, of purity in all domains of life.

Ashoka

There is the Truth where Love and Right-eousness are.

Buddhist Text

Compassion and love, behold the true religion!

Ashoka

Love towards all beings is the true religion.

Jatakamala

I do not know which of the religious leaders is right, nor is it possible for me to know it with any certainty. But I know pertinently that the best I can do is to develop love in myself and about that it is impossible for me to doubt. I cannot doubt it because in developing my love my happiness increases.

Tolstoy

There is no fear in love, but perfect love casteth out fear.

John

Man, if thou wouldst discover in the crowd the friends of God, observe simply those who carry love in their hearts and in their hands.

Angelus Silesius

Renounce without hesitation faith and un-belief.

Farid-uddin Attar

Whoever has his footing firm in love, renounces at one and the same time both religion and unbelief.

Farid-uddin Attar

Light the fire of divine love and destroy all creed and all cult.

Baha-ullah

Believe in the fundamental truth; it is to meditate with rapture on the Everlasting.

Ashwaghosha

The True Religious Man

It is not by shaving the head that one becomes a man of religion; truth and rectitude alone make the true religious man.

Dhammapada

Think not that to seat thyself in gloomy forests, in a proud seclusion, aloof from men, think not that to live on roots and plants and quench thy thirst with the snow shall lead thee to the goal of the final deliverance.

Book of Golden Precepts

Thou shalt see in that spot the mendicant stripped of all resources but with his head troubled by a desire for the possession of the world.

Ahmed Halif

Though the body be adorned with jewels, the heart may have mastered worldly tendencies; he who receives with indifference joy and pain is in possession of the spiritual life even though his external existence be of the world; nor is the garb of the ascetic a protection against sensual thoughts.

Fo-shu-hing-tsan-king

Although the body be robed with the garb of the layman, the soul can raise itself to the highest perfections. The man of the world and the ascetic differ not at all one from the other if both have conquered egoism. So long as the heart is bound by sensual chains, all external signs of asceticism are a vanity.

Fo-shu-hing-tsan-king

There is no difference between a man of the world and a solitary if both have conquered the illusion of the ego; but if the heart is a slave to the desires of the senses, the external signs of self-control serve no useful object.

Fo-shu-hing-tsan-king

A solitary may miss his goal and a man of the world become a sage.

Fo-shu-hing-tsan-king

A gay liver who spreads gladness around him, is better than the devotee who fasts all the year round. Fasting is a merit in the man who distributes his good to the needy; otherwise what mortification is it to take in the evening a meal you have abstained from during the day?

Saadi

Is it such a fast that I have chosen? a day for a man to afflict his soul? is it to bow down his head as a bulrush and to spread sackcloth and ashes under him? wilt thou call this a fast and an acceptable day to the Lord? Is not this the fast that I have chosen? to loose the bonds of wickedness, to undo the heavy burdens, and to let the oppressed go free, and that ye break every yoke? Is it not to deal thy bread to the hungry, and that thou bring the poor that are cast out to thy house? when thou seest the naked, that thou cover him and that thou hide not thyself from thine own kind? Then shall thy light break forth as the morning and thy health shall spring forth speedily.

Isaiah

To take neither wine nor meat is to fast

ceremonially, it is not the heart's fasting which is to maintain in oneself the one thought.

Chuang Tse

And this shall be the true manner of thy fasting that thy life shall be void of all iniquity.

The Pastor of Hermas

The man whose soul aspires to the Eternal cannot give thought to such silly questions as that of daivic food, that is to say, a simple vegetarian diet, and for him who does not desire to attain to the Eternal, beef is as good as daivic food.

Ramakrishna

It is not eating meat that makes a man impure; it is anger, intemperance, egoism, hypocrisy, disloyalty, envy, ostentation, vanity, pride; it is to take pleasure in the society of those who perpetrate injustice.

Amaghanda Sutta

It is not the eating of meat that makes a man

THE TRUE RELIGIOUS MAN **243**

impure; it is to be hard, calumnious, disloyal, without compassion, proud, avaricious, giving no part of one's possessions to another.

Amaghanda Sutta

To be malevolent and violent, a slanderer and unfaithful, without compassion, arrogant and greedy to the point of not giving anything what-soever to others, it is that and not the eating of meat that makes a man impure.

Amaghanda Sutta

The man who does not control himself in his conduct with living beings and who directs all his thoughts towards humiliating them after despoil-ing them of their goods, he who is wicked, cruel, violent, without respect, to him and not to the meat-eater should be applied the stigma of impurity.

Amaghanda Sutta

They who torture living beings and feel no compassion towards them, them regard as impure.

Amaghanda Sutta

Neither abstinence from meat and fish, nor mendicancy, nor the shaven head or the matted locks, nor mortifications of the body, nor garments of a special colour, nor the adoration of a god can purify the man who is still a prey to illusion.

Pali Canon

*
**

He whose mind is utterly purified from soil, as heaven is pure from stain and the moon from dust, him indeed I call a man of religion.

Buddhist Text

He whose mind is utterly pure from all evil as the Sun is pure of stain and the moon of soil, him indeed I call a man of religion.

Udanavagga

He who practises wisdom without anger or covetousness, who fulfils with fidelity his vows and lives master of himself, he is indeed a man of religion.

Buddhist Text

He who watches over his body, his speech, his whole self, who is full of serenity and joy, possesses a spirit unified and finds satisfaction in solitude, he is indeed a man of religion.

Buddhist Text

He who has perfectly mastered himself in thought and speech and act, he is indeed a man of religion.

Buddhist Text

He who puts away from him all passion, hatred, pride and hypocrisy, who pronounces words instructive and benevolent, who does not make his own what has not been given to him, who without desire, covetousness, impatience, knows the depths of the Permanent, he is indeed a man of religion.

Buddhist Text

He who afflicts no living creature, who neither kills nor allows to be killed, him indeed I call a man of religion. Whoever wishes to consecrate himself to the spiritual life, ought not to destroy any life.

Buddhist Text

He who punishes not, kills not, permits not to be killed, who is full of love among those who are full of hate, full of sweetness among those who are full of cruelty, he is indeed a man of religion.

Buddhist Text

He who has conquered the desire of the present life and of the future life, who has vanquished all fear and broken all chains, he is indeed a man of religion.

Buddhist Text

Respect for the Body

Thinkest thou that thy body is nothing when in thee is contained the most perfect world?

Baha-ullah

The human body is the most perfect in the world as the human creature is the most perfect of creatures.

Vivekananda

Your body is an image of heaven and earth confided to your keeping. Your life is the harmony of heaven and earth confided to your keeping.

Chuang Tse

The spirit and the form; sentiment within and symbol without.

Ramakrishna

What purity is for the soul, cleanliness is for the body.

Epictetus

The body is not distinct from the soul but makes of it part and the soul is not distinct from the whole but one of its members.

Farid-uddin Attar

The virtuous cannot but take care for their body, the temple of the soul in which the Eternal manifests Himself or which has been consecrated by His coming.

Ramakrishna

One should maintain the vigour of the body in order to preserve that of the mind.

Vauvenargues

It is important to preserve the body's strength and health, for it is our best instrument. Take care that it is strong and healthy, you possess no better instrument. Imagine that it is as strong as steel and that thanks to it you travel over this ocean of life. The weak will never attain to liberation; put off all weakness, tell your body that it is robust, your intelligence that it is strong, have in yourself a boundless faith and hope.

Vivekananda

There exist two extremes, O my brothers, to which he who aspires to liberation should never abandon himself. One of these extremes is the continual seeking after the satisfaction of the passions and the sensuality; that is vile, coarse, debasing and fatal, that is the road of the children of this world. The other extreme is a life consecrated to mortifications and asceticism; that is full of sorrow, suffering and inutility. Alone the middle path which the Perfect has discovered, avoids these two blind-alleys, accords clear-sightedness, opens the intelligence and conducts to liberation, wisdom and perfection.

Mahavagga

If we walk in the path of true wisdom avoiding the two errors (asceticism and mortifications and the sensual life) we shall attain to the highest perfection. If religion consisted solely in mortifications and asceticism, it could never lead us to Peace.

Fo-shu-hing-tsan-king

Even as the hard Kusha-grass tears the hand which knows not how to seize it, so a misplaced asceticism leads to the lower life.

Dhammapada

Temperance

Let us, who are of the day, be sober.

I Thessalonians

Let us not give ourselves up to excesses.

Shih Ching

Let us watch at the gates of our senses. Let us be moderate in all that regards our nourishment; let us vow ourselves to vigilance and be armed with an intelligence that no fumes have veiled.

Majjhima Nikaya

Be sober, be vigilant.

I Peter

Take heed unto yourselves lest at any time your hearts be overcharged with surfeiting and drunkenness.

Luke

Let us walk, as in the day, not in rioting and drunkenness.

Romans

Master the body; be temperate in food and eat only at opportune moments.

Fo-shu-hing-tsan-king

Giving all diligence, add to virtue knowledge and to knowledge temperance.

II Peter

Gird up the loins of your mind, be sober.

I Peter

Temperance in Speech

Simonides has said that he never repented of having been silent, but often of having spoken.

Apollonius of Tyana

Let every man be swift to hear, slow to speak.

James

Listen much; speak only to the point.

Bias

Suffer not thy tongue to run before thy thought.

Chilon

Behold how great a matter a little fire kindleth; and the tongue is a fire.

James

For the tongue is a smouldering fire and abuse of speech a mortal poison; and while natural fire consumes bodies, the tongue consumes minds and hearts.

Baha-ullah

Rein thy tongue, be without fanaticism and occupy thyself with following the spiritual path.

Farid-uddin Attar

If any man offend not in word, the same is a perfect man and able also to bridle the whole body.

James

He that keepeth his mouth, keepeth his life.

Proverbs

*
**

Continual circumspection in speech; not to abandon thyself to superfluous words.

Confucius

Avoid foolish contentions.

Titus

Whoever passes his time in discussing the good and bad qualities of others, is wasting his time; for it is time spent not in thinking of his own self or the supreme Self, but of other selves.

Ramakrishna

My son, to pass one's time in debate, is to fight against shadows.

Hermes

But foolish and unlearned discussions avoid, knowing that they engender strife.

II Timothy

If those who do not know were to be silent, discord would collapse.

Socrates

By mere controversy you will never succeed in convincing anyone of his error. When the grace of God descends upon him, each will understand his own errors.

Ramakrishna

So long as the bee is outside the calix of the flower and has not tasted the sweetness of its honey, it flies humming around it; but as soon as it has penetrated within, it drinks noiselessly the nectar. So long as a man disputes and discusses about doctrines and dogmas, he has not yet tasted the nectar of the true faith. When he has tasted it, he becomes tranquil and full of peace.

Ramakrishna

When water is poured into an empty jar, a gurgling noise follows; but when the jar is full, no noise is heard. So the man who has not found the Eternal is full of vain disputes about its existence and attributes; but he who has seen it, enjoys silently the divine bliss.

Ramakrishna

The Law of Work

Why stand ye here all the day idle?

Matthew

The righteous man is always active.

Shih Ching

The desire of the slothful killeth him.

Proverbs

Idleness like rust destroys much more than work uses up. A key in use is always clean.

Franklin

The hand of an artisan is always pure when it is at work.

Laws of Manu

There is no shame in any work even the

uncleanest. Idleness alone ought to be held
shameful.

Tolstoy

Indolence is an infirmity and continual
idleness a soil.

Uttama Sutta

Wouldst thou abstain from action? It is not
so that thy soul shall obtain liberation.

Book of Golden Precepts

This is a great error to imagine that men can
have a lofty spiritual life when the body remains in
luxury and idleness. The body is ever the first
disciple of the soul.

Thoreau

Doubt, sorrow, dejection, wrath, despair, all
these demons lie in wait for a man and as soon as
he leads an idle life, they attack; the surest protection against them is assiduous physical labour.

As soon as a man sets himself to this task, no demon can approach him or do more than growl from a distance.

Carlyle

Idleness ought to be numbered among the torments of hell, and it has been placed among the joys of paradise.

Montaigne

The true disciple rejects enervation and idleness; he is delivered from careless lassitude. Loving the light, intelligent and clear of vision he purifies his heart of all carelessness and idleness.

Majjhima Sutta

Go to the ant, thou sluggard; consider her ways and be wise.

Proverbs

Sincerity

Speak always the truth and cultivate harmony.

Li Chi

Speak ye the truth.

Dhammapada

Love the truth and peace.

Zacharias

Have your loins girt about with truth.

Ephesians

Constantly observe sincerity and fidelity and good faith.

Confucius

Hold in horror dissimilation and all hypocrisy.

Fo-shu-hing-tsan-king

Wherefore laying aside all malice and all guile and hypocrisy and envy and all evil speaking.

I Peter

Putting away lying, speak every man truth with his neighbour: for we are members one of another.

Ephesians

Ye shall not steal, neither deal falsely, neither lie one to another.

Leviticus

Lie not one to another.

Colossians

Let your yea be yea and your nay, nay.

James

Never lie; for to lie is infamous.

Zend-Avesta

Put away from thee a forward mouth and perverse lips, put away from speaking guile.

Proverbs

Keep thy tongue from evil and thy lips from speaking guile.

Psalms

Let thy tongue be the instrument of truth. Be ever true in all that thou shall speak and permit not to thy tongue a lie.

Phocylides

My lips shall not speak wickedness nor my tongue utter deceit.

Job

A dumb man's tongue is better than the liar's.

Turkish Proverb

Lying words are unworthy of a disciple, for his aspiration should be sincere and straightforward and knavish and flattering words are kin to witchcraft. The man who occupies himself with spiritual questions, ought not to proffer any such utterances.

Fo-shu-tsan-king

Nothing is superior to truthfulness, nor anything more terrible than falsehood.

Mahabharata

Lying is for slaves; a freeman speaks the truth.

Apollonius of Tyana

Free from the happiness desired by slaves, delivered from the gods and their adoration, fearless and terrible, grand and solitary is the will of the man of truth.

Nietzsche

By whom is this world conquered? By the patient and truthful man.

Prashnottaratrayamala

The more a man is truthful, the more he is divine; unconquerableness, immortality, the greatness of the godhead enter into a man along with truthfulness.

Emerson

Sincerity, a profound, grand, ingenuous sincerity is the first characteristic of all men who are in any way heroic.

Carlyle

I meet the sincere man with sincerity and the insincere also with sincerity.

Lao Tse

When we are alone, we must act with the same sincerity as if ten eyes observed and ten fingers pointed to us.

Tseng Tse

He who acts according to what he holds to be the law of life, — he alone knows the law of life.

Tolstoy

Whoever does not seek out clearly what is the true good, cannot correct himself with sincerity and does not arrive at true perfection.

Confucius

If every man dared speak frankly and highly what he thinks, he would abide always in the reality. How unhappy we make ourselves by striving to hide our nature.

Antoine the Healer

Let us never lose sight of this, my brothers, that when we depart from sincerity, we depart from the Truth.

Antoine the Healer

The eternal Truth shall never be attained by him who is not entirely truthful in his speech.

Ramakrishna

Uprightness

Put always in the first rank uprightness of heart and fidelity.

Confucius

Unto the upright there ariseth light in the darkness.

Psalms

Purity and peace make men upright.

Lao Tse

If the mind makes a practice of rectitude in its thinking, there is no evil that can make entrance into it.

Fo-shu-hing-tsan-king

Upright and sincere is the virtue of the man who directs well his mind.

Lao Tse

An upright nature and true purification is for each the uprightness of his nature.

Zend-Avesta

As one washes the hand with the hand, so uprightness is purified by uprightness. Where there is uprightness, there there is wisdom and where there is wisdom, there there is uprightness, and the wisdom of the upright man, the uprightness of the wise man are of all wisdom and rectitude those which bring in this world the greatest peace.

Sonadanda Sutta

Affirm thy heart in the uprightness of a good conscience; for thou shalt have no more faithful counsellor.

Ecclesiasticus

The good things of this world perish but the treasures won by a life of uprightness are imperishable.

Fo-shu-hing-tsan-king

There is no happiness apart from rectitude.

Buddhist Text

An upright life tastes calm repose by night and by day; it is penetrated with a serene felicity.

Buddhist Text

The simple and upright man is as strong as if he were a great host.

Lao Tse

When I return upon myself and find the heart upright, although my adversaries may be a thousand or ten thousand, I would march without fear on the enemy.

Meng Tse

The man full of uprightness is happy here below, sweet is his sleep by night and by day his heart is radiant with peace.

Buddhist Text

The straight way is the love of the infinite essence.

Baha-ullah

Justice

To do justice and judgment is more acceptable to the Lord than sacrifice.

Proverbs

Blessed are they who hunger and thirst after righteousness, for they shall be filled.

Matthew

Blessed are they who are persecuted for righteousness' sake.

Matthew

The superior man enacts equity, and justice is the foundation of all his deeds.

Confucius

He that followeth after righteousness and mercy, findeth life, righteousness and honour.

Proverbs

The holiness of justice is the health of the soul; it is more precious than heaps of gold and silver.

Ecclesiasticus

All virtues are comprised in justice; if thou art just, thou art a man of virtue.

Theognis

If a man do that which is lawful and right... and hath not oppressed any, but hath restored to the debtor his pledge, hath spoiled none by violence, hath given his bread to the hungry and hath covered the naked with a garment, — he that hath not given forth upon usury, neither hath taken any increase, ... he is just.

Ezekiel

He that is faithful in that which is least is faithful also in much: and he that is unjust in the least is unjust also in much.

Luke

Sow to yourselves in righteousness, reap in mercy, break up your fallow ground.

Hosea

Render unto all men that which is their due.

Corinthians

He that soweth iniquity, shall reap vanity.

Proverbs

They that plough iniquity and sow wickedness, reap the same.

Job

The sinner sins against himself, for he makes himself evil.

Marcus Aurelius

As food mixed with poison, so is abhorrent to me a prosperity soiled by injustice.

Jatakamala

I put on righteousness and it clothed me; my justice was my robe and my diadem.

Job

Serenity

Rejoice evermore.

I Thessalonians

Sorrow is a form of Evil.

Hermes

A merry heart doeth good like a medicine.

Proverbs

Give not up thy heart to sorrow, for it is a sister to distrust and wrath.

The Shepherd of Hermes

Let not thy heart give way to discouragement.

Ecclesiasticus

A man should be glad of heart. If you have

joy no longer, find out where you have fallen into error.

Tolstoy

*
**

There is no happiness so great as peace of mind.

Dhammapada

If Paradise is not within thee, thou shalt never enter into it.

Angelus Silesius

If the discontented man were plunged into the joys of heaven, disquietude would still gnaw at his heart, because precisely contentment is not within him.

Fo-shu-hing-tsan-king

Contentment, internal peace, dominion over oneself, purity, compassion, affectionate words and consideration for friends are seven sorts of fuel which keep alive the flame of happiness.

Mahabharata

Knowledge of God has entered into us and at once ignorance disappears. The knowledge of joy arrives and before her, my son, sorrow shall flee away to those who can still feel her sting.

Hermes

Approach unto wisdom like one who tilleth and soweth and await in peace its excellent fruits.

Ecclesiasticus

There is no peace for the man who is troubled with thought for the future, makes himself unhappy before even unhappiness comes to him and claims to assure till the end of his life his possession of the objects to which he is attached.

Seneca

Give not thy heart over to anxieties.

Mahabharata

Which of you by taking thought can add one cubit to his stature.

Luke

Take no thought for your life, what ye shall eat, nor for your body, what ye shall put on.

Luke

Take no thought for the morrow; for the morrow shall take thought for the things of itself. Sufficient unto the day is the evil thereof.

Matthew

Let not your heart be troubled, neither let it be afraid.

John

Peace be unto you.

John

Equality of Soul

I have learned, in whatever state I am, therewith to be content, both to abound and to suffer need.

Philippians

The man who has conquered himself and is tranquillised, remains fixed in his highest self, whether in pleasure or pain, in honour or in disgrace.

Bhagavad Gita

They have conquered the creation, whose mind is settled in equality.

Bhagavad Gita

He is the happy man whose soul is superior to all happenings.

Seneca

All the accidents of life can be turned to our profit.

Seneca

In all things to do what depends on oneself and for the rest to remain firm and calm.

Epictetus

It is no use being in a rage against things, that makes no difference to them.

Marcus Aurelius

When we can draw from ourselves all our felicity, we find nothing vexatious to us in the order of Nature.

Cicero

True philosophy is beyond all the attacks of things.

Apollonius of Tyana

Truly, man has no retreat more tranquil and less troubled than that which he finds in his own soul, especially if he carries in it those truths to which it is enough to turn to acquire in a moment an absolute quietude.

Marcus Aurelius

The mind which studies is not disquieted.

Lao Tse

The superior man must always remain himself in all situations of life.

Chung Yung

Wherever they may be, upright men remain what they are in themselves. The desire of enjoyment can draw no word from the virtuous. In possession of happiness or in prey to misfortune the wise show neither pride nor dejection.

Dhammapada

Not overjoyed at gaining what is pleasant,

nor disturbed, overtaken by what is unpleasant.

Bhagavad Gita

Like a piece of water that is deep, calm and limpid, having ears only for the precepts of the law the wise live in a complete serenity.

Dhammapada

For if man moves among sensible objects with the senses delivered from liking and dislike and obedient to his self, he attains to serenity. By serenity is born the slaying of all sorrows, for when the heart is serene, the intelligent mind soon comes to its poise.

Bhagavad Gita

A mind which remains calm in the midst of the vicissitudes of life, delivered from preoccupations, liberated from passion, dwelling in serenity — that is a great blessing.

Mahamangala Sutta

A calm heart is the life of the body.

Proverbs

A man of understanding is of an excellent spirit.

Proverbs

The good man remains calm and serene.

Shih Ching

The principle of supreme purity is in repose, in perfect calm.

Huai-nan Tse

The perfection of virtue consists in a certain equality of soul and of conduct which should remain unalterable.

Seneca

The wise in joy and in sorrow depart not from equality of their souls.

Buddhist Text

What is the sign of a man settled in the fixity of his soul and his understanding? When he casts from him all desires that come to the mind, satisfied in himself and with himself, when his mind is undisturbed in pain and without desire in pleasure, when liking and fear and wrath have passed away from him, then a man is fixed in his understanding. He who is unaffected in all things by good or by evil happening, neither rejoices in them nor hates, in him wisdom is established.

Bhagavad Gita

Thus the sage, always equal, awaits the command of destiny, while the vulgar throw themselves into a thousand dangers in a search for happiness at any price.

Confucius

The sage is always at peace; thus his mentality is equally in equilibrium and at ease. His mind is simple and pure, his soul is not subject to lassitude.

Lao Tse

The sage is happy everywhere, the whole earth is his. Nowhere and in no situation is the sage dissatisfied with his condition.

Confucius

He who consecrates his life to spiritual perfection, cannot be ill-content; for what he desires is always in his power.

Pascal

Nothing here below should trouble the sage.

Bhagavad Gita

When you have made progress in wisdom, you will find no situation troublesome to you; every condition will be happy.

Plutarch

In rest shall you be saved, in quietness and confidence shall be your strength.

Isaiah

There is nothing here that is stable, let this truth be ever present to you and you will not let yourselves be transported by joy in prosperity nor cast down by sorrow in disgrace.

Isocrates

Therefore, considering with a firm heart the way of the spirit, renounce the trust which made you see something durable in the cause of joy and sorrow and return into calm.

Bhagavata Purana

Action like inaction can find a place in thee; if thy body agitates itself, let thy mind be calm, let thy soul be limpid as a mountain lake.

Book of Golden Precepts

When water is calm, it reflects objects like a mirror. This tranquillity, this perfect level is the model for the sage. If water is transparent when it is in perfect repose, much more so is the intellectual essence. The heart of the sage in perfect repose is the mirror of heaven and of earth and of all existences.

Chuang Tse

Patience

Even as the high mountain-chains remain immobile in the midst of the tempest, so the true sage remains unshaken amidst praise and blame.

Dhammapada

He who aspires to the true and eternal glory cares nothing for the glory of the age. He who is indifferent to praise or blame enjoys a great serenity of spirit.

Thomas à Kempis

Let men blame him or praise, let fortune enter his house or go forth from it, let death come to him today or late, the man of firm mind never deviates from the straight path.

Bhartrihari

The man who knows Tao is inaccessible to favour as to disgrace, to profit as to loss, to honour as to ignominy.

Lao Tse

The just suffer injury without returning it; they hear reproach without replying; they act only out of love and keep the serenity of their soul in the midst of torments.

Maimonides

Wherefore, O my brothers, if men blame you, condemn you, persecute or attack you, you shall not be indignant, you shall not be discouraged and your spirit shall not be cast down.

Buddhist Text

Be indifferent to the praise and blame of men; consider it as if the croakings of frogs.

Ramakrishna

Fear not the reproach of men, neither be ye afraid of their revilings.

Isaiah

Fear not them which kill the body but are not able to kill the soul.

Matthew

Count it all joy when ye fall into diverse temptations, knowing this that the trying of your faith worketh patience.

James

Blessed is the man that endureth temptation.

James

Is it asked, who is the most excellent of the strong? I reply, it is he who possesses patience.

Sutra in Forty-two Articles

The anvil of the blacksmith remains unshaken under numberless blows of the hammer; so should a man endure with unshaken patience all the ordeals and persecutions which may come upon him.

Ramakrishna

Patience is an invincible breast-plate.

Chinese Buddhist Scripture

If you do not cover yourself on every side with the shield of patience, you will not remain long without wounds.

Thomas à Kempis

Possess your souls in patience.

St. Paul

Your peace shall be in a great patience.

Thomas à Kempis

Rejoicing in hope, patient in tribulation.

Romans

Behold, we count them happy who endure.

James

Patience is sweeter than very honey, by this understand how useful it is to the soul that possesses it.

The Shepherd of Hermes

Be patient, as one who fears no check and does not court success. Fix the gaze of thy soul on the star of which thou art the ray, the flaming star which burns in the obscure depths of the eternal, in the limitless fields of the unknown.

Book of Golden Precepts

Make pain and pleasure, loss and gain, victory and defeat equal to thee, then turn thyself to the battle, so shalt thou have no sin.

Bhagavad Gita

Thou canst live without constraint in profoundest peace of heart, even if all men clamoured against thee what they will, even if wild beasts tore the members of this nature in which thou art enveloped.

Marcus Aurelius

When the water of the fetid pool and the glorious Ganges shall appear to thy eyes as one, when the sound of the flute and the clamour of this crowd shall have no longer any difference to thy ear, then shalt thou attain to the divine Wisdom.

Ramakrishna

***
***

In the day of prosperity be joyful, but in the day of adversity consider.

Ecclesiastes

How shall thy patience be crowned, if it is never tried?

Thomas à Kempis

It is by suffering and troubles that it is given us to acquire little portions of that wisdom which is not learned in books.

Gogol

Men who possess virtue, wisdom, prudence, intelligence have generally been formed in tribulations.

Meng Tse

When Tien wills to give a man a great mission, he begins by proving in bitterness the intentions of his heart. He fatigues his muscles and his bones by painful labours. He lets him suffer hunger. He exposes his person to needs and privations. Finally, he ruins his enterprises. Thereby he stimulates his heart, fortifies his being and gives him an energy without which the man could not accomplish his task. Tribulations produce life; repose and pleasures engender wretchedness and death.

Meng Tse

Others had trials of mockings and scourgings, yea, moreover of bonds and imprisonment: they were stoned, they were sawn asunder, were tortured, were slain with the sword; they wandered about in sheepskins and goatskins, being destitute, afflicted, tormented, of whom the world was not worthy: they wandered in deserts and in mountains and in dens and caves of the earth.

Hebrews

Tribulation worketh patience, and patience experience, and experience hope.

Romans

Only by hope can one attain to unhoped-for things.

Heraclitus

Perseverance

Man can only be happy by the fruit of the labour which he spends on his self-improvement.

Antoine the Healer

From the most exalted in position to the humblest and obscurest of men all have one equal duty, to correct incessantly and improve themselves.

Confucius

One should be careful to improve himself continually.

Shu Ching

To think one is sufficiently virtuous is to lose hold of virtue.

Shu Ching

When one ceases to gain, one begins to lose.

What matters is not to advance quickly, but to be always advancing.

Plutarch

The advance each individual can make corresponds to the excellence he has been able to acquire, and he can only approach his goal by virtue of his self-preparation.

Farid-uddin Attar

When he is animated by a certain desire and by hope, man ought not to shrink from risking his life. He ought not to halt for a moment in his quest, nor to remain an instant in inaction. If he halts, he will be violently rejected far from the road.

Farid-uddin Attar

The aspirant to the true knowledge, if he does not halt in his progress after acquiring certain extraordinary and supernatural powers, becomes in the end rich in the eternal knowledge of the truth.

Ramakrishna

I count not myself to have apprehended, but this one thing I do, forgetting those things which are behind and reaching forth unto those things which are before: I press towards the mark for the prize.

Philippians

*
**

To the persevering and the firm nothing is difficult.

Lun Yu

For all things difficult to acquire the intelligent man works with perseverance.

Lao Tse

Whoso seeketh with diligence, he shall find.

Baha-ullah

There are who do not study or who, though they study, make no progress; let them not be discouraged. There are who put no questions or, when they do, cannot seize well the sense of the reply; let them not be discouraged. There are who can distinguish nothing or only confusedly; let them not be discouraged. There are who do not practise or have no solidity in their practice; let them not be discouraged. What another would do in one step, they will do in a hundred; what another would do in ten, they will do in a thousand. Assuredly, any man who follows this rule, however poorly enlightened he may be, will acquire intelligence and, however weak he may be, will acquire strength.

Confucius

With time and patience the mulberry leaf becomes satin.

Persian Proverb

The soul like the body accepts by practice whatever habit one wishes it to contract.

Socrates

Consecrate yourselves to the purification of

your own minds. Be vigilant, be persevering, be attentive, be thoughtful for your own salvation.

Mahaparinibbana Sutta

He that shall endure unto the end, the same shall be saved.

Matthew

In perseverance ye shall possess your souls.

Luke

But let perseverance have her perfect work that ye may be perfect and entire, wanting nothing.

James

He who sowed sparingly, shall reap also sparingly, and he who sowed bountifully, shall reap also bountifully.

II Corinthians

In due season we shall reap, if we faint not.

Galatians

Let us lay aside every weight and run with patience the race that is set before us.

Hebrews

The pilgrim should never be discouraged; though he should struggle for a hundred thousand years without success to behold the beauty of the Beloved, still he should not give way to despair.

Baha-ullah

It is he who is never discouraged who greatens and tastes the eternal joy.

Mahabharata

If thou hast attempted and failed, O indomitable warrior, yet lose not courage; fight and return to the charge still and always.

Book of Golden Precepts

A just man falleth seven times and riseth up again.

Proverbs

If thy first endeavour to find the Eternal bears no fruit, lose not courage. Persevere and at last thou shalt obtain the divine grace.

Ramakrishna

Be persevering as one who shall last for ever.

Book of Golden Precepts

Vigilance

Let him that thinketh he standeth take heed lest he fall.

Corinthians

It is needful to watch over oneself.

Shu Ching

Sleep not until thou hast held converse with thyself.

Chinese Maxim

Nothing is more evident to the sage than the things hidden in the secrecy of his consciousness, nothing more manifest than the subtle causes of his actions. Therefore the superior man watches attentively over the secret inspirations of his conscience.

Tsu Tse

In the man who keeps no watch over his

conduct, desire extends itself like a creeper. It wanders hither and thither like the monkey running in the forest after a fruit.

Dhammapada

He whose thought spills not itself to this side or that, whose mind is not tormented, who is not anxious any more about good than about evil, for him there is no fear, for he watches.

Dhammapada

By zeal, by vigilance, by peace of soul the sage can make himself as an island which the waves cannot overflow.

Dhammapada

Be watchful, divest yourself of all neglectfulness; follow the path.

Buddhist Maxim

Watch diligently over yourselves, let not negligence be born in you.

Fo-shu-hing-tsan-king

In all circumstances be wakeful.

Baha-ullah

A half attention prepares the way for new illusions and allows the old to grow. By a sustained attention prevent the birth of new errors and destroy the old.

Majjhima Nikaya

Watch with care over your heart and give not way to heedlessness; practise conscientiously every virtue and let not there be born in you any evil inclination.

Buddhist Maxim

Above all things avoid heedlessness; it is the enemy of all virtues.

Fo-shu-hing-tsan-king

The demons become his companions who abandons himself to heedlessness.

Fo-shu-hing-tsan-king

He who was heedless and has become vigilant, shines over the darkened world like a moon in cloudless heavens.

Udanavagga

Energy

Energetically resolved on the search, they must pass without ceasing from negligence to the world of effort.

Baha-ullah

Very weak are our efforts for the discovery of such great blessings, but when we arrive at them, we are recompensed by the felicity of our conscience.

Hermes

Nature has given us strengths in sufficiency, if only we choose to avail ourselves of them and if we collect and employ them all to our profit instead of turning them against ourselves. Our ill will is the cause of what we attribute to a pretended impossibility.

Seneca

If a thing is difficult for thee, imagine not

therefore that it is impossible to man; but if a thing is possible and proper to man, think that it is accessible to thee also.

Marcus Aurelius

Many say with an appearance of humility, "I am even as an earthworm crawling in the dust..."; so always believing themselves to be earthworms, they become in time feeble as the worm. Let not discouragement enter into thy heart; despair is for all the great enemy of our progress. What a man thinks himself to be, that he in fact becomes.

Ramakrishna

In India the healers by faith command their sick to repeat with absolute conviction the words, "There is no malady in me, sickness is not." The sick man repeats and, so mentally denied, his malady disappears. Thus if you believe yourself to be mortally weak, you find yourself actually in that condition. Know and believe that you can have an immense power, and the power will come to you in the end.

Ramakrishna

It is bad for man to think that he is without sin and has no need to struggle with himself; but it is quite as bad for him to think that he is born in sin, condemned to die under a load of sins and that it would be of no use for him to struggle to rid himself of them. Both these errors are equally fatal.

Tolstoy

True good can only be obtained by our effort towards spiritual perfection and this effort is always in our power.

Epictetus

Who is the enemy? Lack of energy.

Prashnottaratrayamala

Nothing is more dangerous for man than negligence.

Mahabharata

A single day of life of the man who stimulates himself by an act of energy, is of more value than a hundred years passed in nonchalance and indolence.

Buddhist Text

Indolence is a soil.

Buddhist Text

The disciple has rejected indolence and indolence conquers him not; loving the light, intelligent, clearly conscient, he purifies his heart of all laxness and all lassitude.

Buddhist Text

I know nothing which engenders evil and weakens good so much as carelessness; in the uncaring evil appears at once and effaces good. I know nothing which engenders good and weakens evil so much as energy; in the energetic good at once appears and evil vanishes.

Buddhist Text

Carelessness is not proper even for the worldling who derives vanity from his family and his riches; how much less for a disciple who has proposed to himself for his goal to discover the path of liberation!

Fo-shu-hing-tsan-king

Whoso has been careless and has conquered his carelessness, whoso having committed errors concentrates his whole will towards good, shines on the darkened world like the moon in a cloudless sky.

Chinese Buddhist Saying

Use all your forces for endeavour and leave no room for carelessness.

Buddhist Text

Endeavour with your whole energy and leave no place for carelessness.

Fo-shu-hing-tsan-king

Zealous and not slothful; fervent in spirit.

Romans

Thyself stimulate and direct thyself; thus self-protected and clairvoyant thou shalt live happy.

Dhammapada

Arise and be not slothful! Follow the straight path! He who walks, lives happy in this world and in those beyond.

Dhammapada

For such a man, one who neglects no effort to set himself from now in the ranks of the best, is a priest, a minister of the gods, a friend of Him who dwells within him.

Marcus Aurelius

Firmness

No compromises; to live resolutely in integrity, plenitude and beauty.

Goethe

The firmness of our resolution gives the measure of our progress and a great diligence is needed if one wishes to advance.

Thomas à Kempis

Circumstances, though they attack obstinately the man who is firm, cannot destroy his proper virtue, — firmness.

Bhartrihari

Stand firm therefore, having your loins girt about with truth and having on the breastplate of righteousness.

Ephesians

Be firm in the accomplishment of your duties, the great and the small.

Buddhist Text

Be ye steadfast, immovable.

I Corinthians

When you have seen your aim, hold to it, firm and unshakeable.

Dhammapada

Turn not thy head from this path till thou art led to its end; keep ever near to this door till it is opened. Let not thy eyes be shut; seek well and thou shalt find.

Farid-uddin Attar

Seek wisdom carefully and she shall be uncovered to thee, and when once thou hast seen her, leave her not.

Ecclesiasticus

Hold that fast which thou hast, that no man take thy crown.

Revelations

Be thou faithful unto death.

Revelations

Boldness

Watch ye, stand fast, quit you like men, be strong.

I Corinthians

Be strong and of a good courage; fear not.

Deuteronomy

Lift up the hands which hang down and the feeble knees.

Hebrews

Be strong; fear not.

Isaiah

Man's first duty is to conquer fear.

Carlyle

A man's deeds are slavish, his very thoughts

false, so long as he has not succeeded in putting fear under his feet.

Carlyle

In heaven fear is not.

Katha Upanishad

The sage here surpasses God. God fears nothing by the benefit of his nature; the sage fears nothing, but by the sole strength of his spirit. This indeed is great, to have the weakness of a mortal and yet the fearlessness of a god.

Seneca

It is only the coward who appeals always to destiny and never to courage.

Ramayana

Fortune fears the brave soul; she crushes the coward.

Seneca

He who shows not zeal where zeal should be shown, who young and strong gives himself up to indolence, who lets his will and intelligence sleep, that do-nothing, that coward shall not find the way of the perfect knowledge.

Dhammapada

It needs a lion-hearted man to travel the extraordinary path; for the way is long and the sea is deep.

Farid-uddin Attar

There are pearls in the depths of the ocean, but one must dare all the perils of the deep to have them. So is it with the Eternal in the world.

Ramakrishna

*
**

Fear none of those things which thou shalt suffer.

Revelations

The more thou shalt advance, the more thy feet shall encounter bog and morass. The path which thou walkest, is lighted by only one fire, even the light of the audacity which burns in thy heart. The more thou shalt dare, the more thou shalt obtain.

Book of Golden Precepts

Go in this thy might.

Judges

Be not afraid, only believe.

Mark

All things are possible to him that believeth.

Mark

I will trust and not be afraid.

Isaiah

Simplicity and Modesty

Let not therefore the wise man glory in his wisdom, neither let the mighty man glory in his might, let not the rich man glory in his riches.

Jeremiah

A man's pride shall bring him low, but honour shall uphold the humble in spirit.

Proverbs

Pride goeth before destruction, but before honour is humility.

Proverbs

Whosoever exalteth himself shall be abased, and he that humbleth himself shall be exalted.

Luke

If you give to a man all riches and all might and he looks upon himself with the same humility as before, than that man far surpasses other human beings.

Meng Tse

All the splendour of outward greatness has no lustre for men who are in search of the Spirit. The greatness of men of the Spirit is obnoxious to the rich, the kings, the conquerors and all the men of the flesh.

Pascal

Such are they who have not acquired self-knowledge, men who vaunt their science, are proud of their wisdom, vain of their riches.

Ramakrishna

Man is good when he raises very high his divine and spiritual "I", but frightful when he wishes to exalt above men his fleshly "I" vain, ambitious and exclusive.

Tolstoy

All other vanities can be gradually extinguished, but the vanity of the saint in his saintliness is difficult indeed to banish.

Ramakrishna

This is a great fault in men, to love to be the models of others.

Meng Tse

To be a man of worth and not to try to look like one is the true way to glory.

Socrates

The supreme virtue does not consider itself a virtue and that is why it is virtue: the inferior positively believes itself to be virtue and that is why it is not virtue.

Lao Tse

Men of superior virtue practise it without thinking of it; those of inferior virtue go about it with intention.

Lao Tse

The man of superior virtue is well pleased in the humblest situation. His heart loves to be deep as the abyss.

Lao Tse

The saint does good and makes not much of it. He accomplishes great things and is not attached to them. He does not wish to let his wisdom appear.

Lao Tse

The saint does not seek to do great things; that is why he is able to accomplish them.

Lao Tse

When one has done great things and made a reputation, one should withdraw out of view.

Lao Tse

The man who has done good does not cry it through the world.

Marcus Aurelius

So long as a man has a little knowledge, he goes everywhere reading and preaching; but when the perfect knowledge has been attained, one ceases from vain ostentation.

Ramakrishna

Only the man who knows that God lives in his soul, can be humble; such a one is absolutely indifferent to what men say of him.

Tolstoy

Take heed that ye do not alms before men, to be seen of them.

Matthew

Make no parade of your wisdom; it is a vanity which costs dear to many. Let wisdom correct your vices, but not attack those of others.

Seneca

Mind not high things, but condescend to

men of low estate. Be not wise in your own conceit.

Romans

I say to every man that is among you, not to think of himself more highly than he ought to think, but to think soberly.

Romans

Be pure, be simple and hold always a just mean.

Shu Ching

Unite always to a great exactitude, uprightness and simplicity of heart.

Shu Ching

Be ye wise as serpents and simple as doves.

Matthew

Be humble if thou wouldst attain to wisdom; be humbler still if thou hast attained to it.

Book of Golden Precepts

Seest thou a man wise in his own conceit? there is more hope of a fool than of him.

Proverbs

Be not proud in thy riches, nor in thy strength, nor in thy wisdom.

Phocylides

If thou givest thyself up to the least pride, thou art no longer master of thyself, thou losest thy understanding as if thou wert drunk with wine.

Farid-uddin Attar

So long as thou livest in the bewilderment and seduction of pride, thou shalt abide far from the truth.

Farid-uddin Attar

Thou hast cleansed thy heart of soil and bled it dry of impure desires. But, O glorious combatant, thy task is not yet done. Build high the wall which shall protect thy mind from pride and satisfaction at the thought of the great work accomplished.

Book of Golden Precepts

Oh, if the heart could become a cradle and God once more a child upon the earth!

Angelus Silesius

SECTION III

THE CONQUEST OF SELF

Disinterestedness

Self-interest is the prolongation in us of the animal. Humanity begins in man with disinterestedness.

Amiel

Disinterestedness is not always understood. Yet is it the foundation of the virtues, without it they could not be practised.

Antoine the Healer

As dawn announces the rising of the sun, so in a man disinterestedness, purity, rectitude forerun the coming of the Eternal.

Ramakrishna

Whoever is rich within and embellished with virtue, seeks not outside himself for glory and riches.

Angelus Silesius

The perfect man does not hunt after wealth.

Confucius

He must content himself with little and never ask for more than he has.

Baha-ullah

The least indigent mortal is the one who desires the least. We have everything we wish when we wish only for what is sufficient.

Seneca

Many things are wanting to indigence, but everything is wanting to greed. A covetous man is useful to none and still less is he of any good to himself.

Seneca

To covet external objects is to defile the mind.

Shu Ching

To work only in the material sense is to increase the load that is crushing us.

Antoine the Healer

We brought nothing into this world and it is certain we can carry nothing out, — and having food and raiment let us be therewith content. But they that will be rich fall into temptation and a snare and into many foolish and hurtful lusts which drown men in destruction and perdition. For the love of money is the root of all evil.

Timothy

*
**

O you who are vain of your mortal possessions, know that wealth is a heavy barrier between the seeker and the Desired.

Baha-ullah

Children of knowledge! the slender eyelash can prevent the eye from seeing; what then must be the effect of the veil of avarice over the eye of the heart!

Baha-ullah

Let your behaviour be without covetousness, and be content with such things as you have.

Hebrews

In vain are you rich if you do not quell your passions; if an insatiable cupidity eats you up, if you are the prey of fears and anxieties, of what use to you is your opulence?

Plutarch

Mortify therefore covetousness, which is idolatry.

Colossians

Set not thy heart upon riches.

Psalms

Let your body be pure, pure your words, pure your thoughts. Free yourselves from the preoccupations of daily life; let not fields, houses, cattle, wealth and worldly goods be your encumbrances. Avoid the anxieties which attend on all things, as one shuns a flaming gulf.

Fo-shu-hing-tsan-king

Labour not for the food which perishes but for that which endures into everlasting life.

John

For where your treasure is, there will your heart be also.

Matthew

*
**

O thou who resumest in thyself all creation, cease for one moment to be preoccupied with gain and loss.

Omar Khayyam

Found not thy glory on power and riches.

Theognis

Vex not thyself to be rich; cease from thy own wisdom. Wilt thou set thy eyes upon that which is not? for riches certainly make themselves wings.

Proverbs

Thou whom all respect, impoverish thyself that thou mayst enter the abode of the supreme riches.

Baha-ullah

Thou shalt leave behind thee the embarrassments with which wealth surrounds thee and thou shalt find the immensity of the spiritual kingdom.

Ahmed Halif

I have never counted as real possessions either treasures or palaces or the places which give us credit and put authority in our hands or the pleasures of which men are slaves.

Cicero

I strive to attain the happiness which does not pass away nor perish and which has not its source in riches or beauty nor depends upon them.

Fo-shu-hing-tsan-king

My joy is in labouring to acquire spiritual wealth; for the riches of this world pass away, but the treasures of our spiritual earnings abide for ever.

Fo-shu-hing-tsan-king

To Renounce Coveting

There is no fire that can equal desire.

Dhammapada

Coveting is without end, but contentment is a supreme felicity; therefore the wise recognise no treasures upon the earth except contentment alone.

Mahabharata

The world is carried away in the torrent of desire, in its eddies there is no soil of safety. Wisdom alone is a solid raft and meditation a firm foothold.

Fo-shu-hing-tsan-king

From coveting is born grief, from coveting is born fear. To be free utterly from desire is to know neither fear nor sorrow.

Dhammapada

When a man shakes from him the clinging yoke of desire, affliction drops away from him little by little as drops of water glide from a lotus-leaf.

Dhammapada

I, such as I am, belong not to myself.... A man should think thus, "All earth is mine," or thus, "All this belongs to others just as well as to myself;" such a man is never afflicted.

Mahabharata

Let him repulse lust and coveting, the disciple who would lead a holy life.

Dhammapada

If a man covets nothing, how shall he fail to do what is just and good?

Shih Ching

The body may be covered with jewels and yet the heart may have mastered all the covetings.

Fo-shu-hing-tsan-king

To Renounce the Fruit of Works

Personal success ought never to be considered the aim of existence.

Bacon

One does not need to hope in order to act, nor to succeed in order to persevere.

William the Silent

The superior man perseveres in the middle path. Even though he remains unknown and the world esteems him not, he feels no regret. The sage alone is capable of such an action.

Tsang Yung

Poor souls are they whose work is for a reward.

Bhagavad Gita

Thou hast a right only to work, but never to its fruits.

Bhagavad Gita

It is impossible for man who has a body to abstain absolutely from all action, but whoever renounces its fruits, is the man of true renunciation.

Bhagavad Gita

He who sees that in inaction there is an act and that in works there can be freedom from the act, is the wise among men.... When a man has given up the fruit of his works and is eternally content and without dependence upon things, then though occupied in works, it is not he that is doing any act.

Bhagavad Gita

When anyone does good without troubling himself for the result, ambition and malevolence pass quickly away from him.

Fo-shu-hing-tsan-king

When the man who does good, ceases to concern himself with the result of his act, ambition and wrath are extinguished within him.

Lalita Vistara

The act done under right rule, with detachment, without liking or dislike, by the man who grasps not at the fruit, that is a work of light.

Bhagavad Gita

A one-minded pursuit of the inner joys kills ambition.

Renan

The Master has said, "To pore over mysterious things and do miracles that I may be cited with honour in future times, this is what I will not do."

Tsang Yung

To Renounce Desire

The difficulties which come to birth in the disciple, are ignorance, egoism, desire, aversion and a tenacious will to existence upon the earth.

Patanjali

There is no better way to cultivate humanity and justice in the heart than to diminish our desires.

Meng Tse

It is good to have what one desires, but it is better to desire nothing more than what one has.

Menedemus

You tell me that good cheer, raiment, riches and luxury are happiness. I believe that the greatest felicity is to desire nothing, and in order to draw near to this supreme happiness, one must habituate oneself to have need of little.

Socrates

O children of desire, cast off your garb of vanities.

Baha-ullah

Renounce your desires and you shall taste of peace.

Thomas à Kempis

So long as man has not thrown from him the load of worldly desire which he carries about with him, he cannot be in tranquillity and at peace with himself.

Ramakrishna

The man in whom all desires disappear like rivers into a motionless sea, attains to peace, not he whom they move to longing. That man whose walk is free from longing, for he has thrown all desires from him, who calls nothing his and has no sense of ego, is moving towards peace.

Bhagavad Gita

Ah! let us live happy without desires among

those who are given up to covetousness. In the midst of men full of desires, let us dwell empty of them.

Dhammapada

*
**

Let us impose upon our desires the yoke of submission to reason, let them be ever calm and never bring trouble into our souls; thence result wisdom, constancy, moderation.

Cicero

The man veritably free is he who, disburdened of fear and desire, is subjected only to his reason.

Fénelon

Whoever prefers to all else his reason, does not enact tragedy, does not bewail himself, seeks neither solitude nor the crowd, but, greatest of all goods, he shall live without desire and without fear.

Marcus Aurelius

When his thought and feeling are perfectly under regulation and stand firm in his Self, then, unmoved to longing by any desire, he is said to be in union with the Self.

Bhagavad Gita

He has read everything, learned everything, practised everything, who has renounced his desires and lives without any straining of hope.

Hitopadesha

*
**

The breath of desire and pleasure so ravages the world that it has extinguished the torch of knowledge and understanding.

Baha-ullah

As the troubled surface of rolling waters cannot reflect aright the full moon, but gives only broken images of it, so the mentality troubled by the desires and passions of the world cannot reflect fully the light of the Eternal.

Ramakrishna

Then is the Eternal seen when the mind is at rest. When the sea of mind is tossed by the winds of desire, it cannot reflect the Eternal and all divine vision is impossible.

Ramakrishna

Man, wouldst thou be a sage, wouldst thou know thyself and know God? First thou shouldst extinguish in thyself the desire of the world.

Angelus Silesius

Desire nothing. Rage not against the unalterable laws of Nature. Struggle only against the personal, the transient, the ephemeral, the perishable.

Book of Golden Precepts

The light of thy spirit cannot destroy these shades of night so long as thou hast not driven out desire from thy soul.

Hindu Saying

When thou art enfranchised from all hate

and desire, then shalt thou win thy liberation.

Dhammapada

Expel thy desires and fears and there shall be no longer any tyrant over thee.

Marcus Aurelius

If thou wouldst be free, accustom thyself to curb thy desires.

Tolstoy

Slay thy desires, O disciple, make powerless thy vices, before thou takest the first step of that solemn journey.

Book of Golden Precepts

Slay desire, but when thou hast slain it, take heed that it arise not again from the dead.

Book of Golden Precepts

Surmount the desires of which gods and men are the subjects.

Uttama Sutta

How canst thou desire anything farther when in thyself there are God and all things?

Angelus Silesius

To Renounce the World

Love cannot be used for the fulfilment of desire, for its nature is renunciation. Renunciation is the renunciation of ritual works and worldly affairs.

Narada Sutra

The insensate enter into the world, seduced by its false splendours. But just as it is easier to get into a net than to escape from it, so is it easier to enter into the world than, having once entered, to renounce it.

Ramakrishna

The man who lives in the bosom of the temptations of the world and attains perfection, is the true hero.

Ramakrishna

A boat can be in the water, but the water ought not to be in the boat. So the aspirant may live in the world, but the world should find no place in him.

Ramakrishna

What is a man profited if he shall gain the whole world, and lose his own soul?

Matthew

Man is in truth a compound of eternity and time. The more he is attached to temporal things and rests in them, the farther he grows from things eternal; they seem to him petty, just as great objects appear small when we see them from a distance, and he can never attain to real peace.

Tauler

Vanity of vanities, all is vanity. What profit hath a man of all his labour which he taketh under the sun?

Ecclesiastes

Is it from without that there can come to a

man the sweetness and the charm of his life? Is it not rather from the wisdom of his virtues that flow as from a happy source his real pleasures and his real joys?

Plutarch

Whoever gives himself up to rational meditations, finds very soon the joy in all that is good. He sees that riches and beauty are impermanent and wisdom the most precious of jewels.

Fo-shu-hing-tsan-king

Youth, beauty, life, riches, health, friends are things that pass; let not the wise man attach himself at all to these.

Mahabharata

When the sage has recognised impermanence, subjection to grief and unreality of substance as the three characteristic qualities of this world, how can his heart own attachment to the things of this world?

Fo-shu-hing-tsan-king

In the Ineffable who is the indivisible and eternal bliss, are centered all pleasure and happiness. Those who enjoy him, can find no attraction to the facile and valueless pleasures of the world.

Ramakrishna

What can he desire in the world who is greater than the world?

St. Cyprian

What joy is there in this world which is everywhere a prey to flames?

Dhammapada

*
**

O disciples, be ye heirs to Truth, not to worldly things.

Majjhima Nikaya

Love not the world, neither the things that are in the world.

John

Seek those things which are above.

Colossians

Covet earnestly the best gifts.

I Corinthians

My son, go back into thy self by disentangling thyself as much as thou mayst from all things; seek purity from things below by detaching thy will and thy heart from the love of sensible objects.

Tauler

Reject passion and attachment, then shall be revealed in thee that which now dwells hidden from thy eyes.

Sutra in Forty-two Articles

Where your treasure is, there will your heart be also.

Matthew

O friend, fill not with mortal thoughts thy heart which is the seat of eternal mysteries.

Baha-ullah

What offering should be made that we may attain to the Eternal? To find the Eternal thou must offer him thy body, thy mind and all thy possessions.

Ramakrishna

No man of war entangleth himself with the affairs of this life.

II Timothy

If you would live tranquil and free, get rid of the habit of all which you can do without.

Tolstoy

Man! renounce all that thou mayst be happy, that thou mayst be free, that thou mayst have thy soul large and great. Carry high thy head,... and thou art delivered from servitude.

Epictetus

So live as if thou hadst at once to say farewell to life and the time yet accorded thee were an unexpected gift.

Marcus Aurelius

Eternity is for all time, but the world only for a moment. Sell not then for that moment thy kingdom of eternity.

Omar Khayyam

To Renounce One's Self

Whosoever has oneness engraven in his heart, forgets all things and forgets himself.

Farid-uddin Attar

It is from the shoot of self-renunciation that there starts the sweet fruit of final deliverance.

Book of Golden Precepts

This liberation is attained by him alone who has understood the lesson of complete disinterestedness and forgetfulness of self.

Ramakrishna

Knowledge is better than practice, concentration excels knowledge, the renunciation of fruits concentration; peace is the immediate result of renunciation.

Bhagavad Gita

To renounce one's self is not to renounce life.

Tolstoy

None can be richer, more powerful, freer than he who knows how to renounce his self and all things.

Thomas à Kempis

To put an end to care for one's self is a great happiness.

Udanavagga

One must begin by annihilating one's self, to be able to kindle within the Flame of existence and be admitted into the paths of Love.

Baha-ullah

Not by work, not by family, not by riches, but by renunciation great beings attain to immortality.

Kaivalya Upanishad

Only he who lives not for himself, does not perish.

Lao Tse

Man, every time he gives up and abandons himself, finds God in the depths of his heart, as if the immutable principle of his abnegation.

Tauler

The individual consciousness by the attempt to measure the Impersonal loses its individual egoism and becomes one with Him.

Ramakrishna

Each being who renounces his self and detaches himself completely from it, hears within this voice and this echo, "I am God."

Gulschen-i-Raz

Totally to renounce one's self is to become God.

Tolstoy

Therefore regard attentively this ocean of impermanence, contemplate it even to its foundation and labour no more to attain but one sole thing, — the kingdom of the Permanent.

Buddhist Text

Deliver yourself from all that is not your self; but what is it that is not your self? The body, the sensations, the perceptions, the relative differentiations. This liberation will lead you to felicity and peace.

Buddhist Text

My brother, a delicate heart is like a mirror; polish it by love and detachment, that the Sun of the Reality may reflect itself in it and the divine Dawn arise.

Baha-ullah

Cut away in thee the love of thyself, even as in autumn thy hand plucks the lotus.

Dhammapada

Root out in thee all love of thyself and all egoism.

Buddhist Text

Above all banish the thought of the "I".

Fo-shu-hing-tsan-king

Thou shalt have given a drop and won the sea, given thy life and won the well-beloved.

Baha-ullah

The Mastery of the Senses

In the man who contemplates the objects of the senses, attachment to them is born, from attachment is born desire, and from desire is born the wrath of desire; from that wrath delusion and from delusion error of the memory in the reason; from the error loss of understanding, and by the loss of understanding he goes to perdition.

Bhagavad Gita

Human souls which have not the intelligence for their guide, are even as animals without reason. Intelligence abandons them to the passions which draw them by the lure of desire; their wraths and their appetites are equally blind and push them towards evil without ever finding satiety.

Hermes

Who is blinder even than the blind? The man of passion.

Buddhist Maxim

When the soul has not self-mastery, one looks and sees not, listens and hears not.

Tseng Tse

Is one, indeed, master of himself when he follows his own caprices?

Farid-uddin Attar

The evildoer is the only slave.

Rousseau

The ignorant is the slave of his passions, the wise man is their master.

Sutra in Forty-two Articles

It is by resisting the passions, not by yielding to them that one finds true peace in the heart.

Thomas à Kempis

By the taming of the senses the intelligence grows.

Mahabharata

Not to tame the senses is to take the road of misery, to conquer them is to enter into the path of well-being. Let each choose of these two roads the one that pleases him.

Hitopadesha

Happy the man who has tamed the senses and is utterly their master.

Buddhist Maxim

A man who has command over his senses and the forces of his being, has a just title to the name of king.

Angelus Silesius

The radiant beings themselves envy him whose senses are mastered like horses well trained by their driver.

Udanavagga

He whose senses have become calm like horses perfectly tamed by a driver, who has rid himself of pride and concupiscence, the gods themselves envy his lot.

Dhammapada

Thus become wise, calm, submitted, passionless, enduring, master of himself, he sees the Self in himself and in all beings. Sin conquers him no more, he conquers sin; sin consumes him no more, he consumes sin.

Brihadaranyaka Upanishad

*
**

Repress then your senses; calm, minds appeased, master your bodies.

Lalita Vistara

Shun agreeable amusements, deliver not yourselves to the pleasures of the senses.

Shu Ching

Renounce pleasure and renounce wrath and observe justice.

Mahabharata

Dearly beloved, I beseech you as strangers and pilgrims, abstain from fleshly lusts which war against the soul.

I Peter

Every one of you should know how to possess his vessel in sanctification and honour, not in the lust of concupiscence.

I Thessalonians

Ye have been called unto liberty; only use not liberty for an occasion to the flesh.

Galatians

Labour to master adversity even as your passions, to which it would be shameful for you to be subjected.

Socrates

Ye have not yet resisted unto blood, striving against sin.

Hebrews

THE MASTERY OF THE SENSES 365

Let not sin therefore reign in your mortal body that ye should obey it in the lusts thereof.

Romans

Let your whole spirit and soul and body be preserved blameless.

I Thessalonians

*
**

At first sin is a stranger in the soul; then it becomes a guest; and when we are habituated to it, it becomes as if the master of the house.

Tolstoy

Thus little by little the enemy invades the soul, if it is not resisted from the beginning.

Thomas à Kempis

By what is man impelled to act sin, though not willing it, as if brought to it by force? It is desire, it is wrath born of the principle of passion, a mighty and devouring and evil thing; know this for the enemy. Eternal enemy of the sage, in the form of desire, it obscures his knowledge and is an insatiable fire. The senses are supreme in the body, above the senses is the mind, higher than the mind is the understanding and higher than the understanding the spiritual Self. Know then that which is higher than the understanding, by the self control thyself and slay this difficult enemy, desire.

Bhagavad Gita

Know that all this is so, but habituate thyself to surmount and conquer thy passions.

Pythagoras

Flee youthful lusts.

II Timothy

If thou hast many vices, thou hast many masters.

Petrarch

Dominate the rush of passion. Yield not to

the impulsion of a turbulent heart; he who is able to calm his heart when passion suddenly inflames it, can be called indeed a skilful driver of the chariot.

Fo-shu-hing-tsan-king

Fear pleasure, it is the mother of grief.

Solon

As a living man abstains from mortal poisons, so put away from thee all defilement.

Buddhist Text

Keep thy heart with all diligence, for out of it are the issues of life.

Proverbs

Keep thyself from all evil in thought, in word, in act. If thou transgress not these three frontiers of wisdom, thou shalt find the way pursued by the saints.

Majjhima Nikaya

The Mastery of Thought

They had gained this supreme perfection, to be totally masters of their thoughts.

Lotus Sutra

To control the mind! How difficult that is! It has been compared, not without good reason, to a mad monkey.

Vivekananda

Hard is the mind to restrain, light, running where it pleases; to subjugate it is a salutary achievement; subjugated it brings happiness.

Dhammapada

The mind is restless, strong, insistent, violently disturbing; to control it I hold to be as difficult as to control the wind.

Bhagavad Gita

Just as a fly settles now on an unclean sore in

the body, not on the offerings consecrated to the gods, so the mind of a worldly man stops for a moment upon religious ideas, but the next it strays away to the pleasures of luxury and lust.

Ramakrishna

On the vacillating, the mobile mind so difficult to hold in, so difficult to master, the man of intelligence imposes a rectitude like the direct straightness which the arrow-maker gives to an arrow.

Dhammapada

So long as the mind is inconstant and inconsequent, it will avail nothing, even though one have a good instructor and the company of the saints.

Ramakrishna

Like a chariot drawn by wild horses is the mind, the man of knowledge should hold it in with an unswerving attention.

Shwetashwatara Upanishad

Each time that the mobile and inconstant mind goes outward, it should be controlled, brought back into oneself and made obedient.

Bhagavad Gita

An evil thought is the most dangerous of all thieves.

Chinese Buddhist Scripture

We hear it said and taught over the whole surface of the earth, "Be good, be good." There is hardly anywhere a child, wherever he is born, to whom one does not say, "Do not steal, do not lie."... But we can only be really helpful to him by teaching him to dominate his thoughts.

Vivekananda

A big tree is at first a slender shoot; a nine-storied tower is raised by first placing a few small bricks; a journey of a thousand leagues begins with a step. Be careful of your thoughts; they are the beginning of your acts.

Lao Tse

Let not worldly thoughts and anxieties disturb the mind.

Ramakrishna

Think no evil thoughts.

Kun Yu

Whatsoever things are true, whatsoever things are honest, whatsoever things are just, whatsoever things are pure, whatsoever things are lovely, whatsoever things are of good report, if there be any virtue and if there be any praise, think on these things.

Philippians

When a thought of anger or cruelty or a bad and unwholesome inclination awakes in a man, let him immediately throw it from him, let him dispel it, destroy it, prevent it from staying with him.

Buddhist Maxim

When the disciple regarding his ideas sees

appear in him bad and unwholesome thoughts, thoughts of covetousness, hatred, error, he should either turn his mind from them and concentrate on a healthy idea, or examine the fatal nature of the thought, or else he should analyse it and decompose it into its different elements, or calling up all his strength and applying the greatest energy suppress it from his mind: so bad and unwholesome thoughts withdraw and disappear, and the mind becomes firm, calm, unified, vigorous.

Buddhist Maxim

We cannot prevent birds from flying over our heads but we can prevent them from making their nests there. So we cannot prevent evil thoughts from traversing the mind, but we have the power not to let them make their nest in it so as to hatch and engender evil actions.

Luther

Let us keep watch over our thoughts.

Fo-shu-hing-tsan-king

When a thought rises in us, let us see whether it has not its roots in the inferior worlds.

Antoine the Healer

So let us accomplish what we know to be upright, let us keep watch over our thoughts so as not to suffer ourselves to be invaded by any pollution. As we sow, so we shall reap.

Fo-shu-hing-tsan-king

The Mastery of Self

The self is the master of the self, what other master wouldst thou have? A self well-controlled is a master one can get with difficulty.

Dhammapada

The self is the master of the self, what other master of it canst thou have? A wise man who has made himself the master of himself, has broken his chains, he has rent the ties of his bondage.

Udanavagga

The self is the master of the self, what other master of it canst thou have? The wise man who has made himself the master of himself, is a world-illumining beacon.

Udanavagga

Good is the mastery of the body, good the

mastery of the speech, good too the mastery of the thought, good the perfect self-mastery.

Majjhima Nikaya

Good is the mastery of the body, good the mastery of the speech, good too the mastery of the mind, good the perfect self-mastery. The disciple who is the master of himself, shall deliver his soul from every sorrow.

Dhammapada

The true treasure is self-mastery; it is the secret wealth which cannot perish.

Nidhikama Sutta

Life is not short if it is filled. The way to fill it is to compel the soul to enjoy its own wealth and to become its own master.

Seneca

Our intelligence ought to govern us as a herdsman governs his goats, cows and sheep, preferring for himself and his herd all that is useful and agreeable.

Philo

A man who cannot command himself, should obey. But there are too those who know how to command themselves, but yet are very far from knowing how also to obey.

Nietzsche

The body of man is a chariot, his mind the driver, his senses the horses. The man of intelligence who keeps watch over himself, travels on his way like an owner of a chariot, happy and contented, drawn by well-trained horses.

Mahabharata

Self-control brings calm to the mind, without it the seed of all the virtues perishes.

Fo-shu-hing-tsan-king

Self-control which lies on a man like a fine

garment, falls away from him who negligently gives himself up to slumber.

Fo-shu-hing-tsan-king

He that hath no rule over his own spirit, is like a city that is broken down and without walls.

Proverbs

One should guard oneself like a frontier citadel well defended without and within.

Dhammapada

Difficult is union with God when the self is not under governance; but when the self is well-subjected, there are means to come by it.

Bhagavad Gita

When the thought of a man is without attachment, when he has conquered himself and is rid of desire, by that renunciation he reaches a supreme perfection of quietude.

Bhagavad Gita

In union by a purified understanding, controlling himself by a firm perseverance, abandoning the objects of the senses, putting away from him all liking and disliking, when one resorts to solitude, lives on little, masters speech and mind and body, ever in meditation and fixed in withdrawal from the desires of the world, when he has loosened from him egoism and violence and pride and lust and wrath and possession, then calm and without thought of self, he is able to become one with the Eternal.

Bhagavad Gita

*
**

By virile activity, by vigilant effort, by empire over himself, by moderation, the sage can make himself an island which the floods shall not inundate.

Dhammapada

He is the wise man who, having once taken up his resolve, acts and does not cease from the labour, who does not lose uselessly his days and who knows how to govern himself.

Mahabharata

The sage should be figured in the image of a robust athlete whom long exercise has hardened, one who can baffle the efforts of the most obstinate enemy.

Seneca

He is the perfect athlete who surmounts temptations and the incline of his nature towards sin and exercises over his mind domination and empire.

Tauler

Who is the wise man? Whosoever is constantly learning something from one man or another. Who is the rich man? Whosoever is contented with his lot. Who is the strong man? Whosoever is capable of self-mastery.

Talmud

If holiness can be compared to any other quality, it is only to strength.

Meng Tse

Strength of character primes strength of intelligence.

Emerson

True strength is to have power over oneself.

Tolstoy

When the spirit has command over the soul, that is strength.

Lao Tse

*
**

The soul spiritual should have command over the soul of sense.

Lao Tse

All souls have within them something soft, cowardly, vile, nerveless, languishing, and if there were only that element in man, there would be nothing so ugly as the human being. But at the same time there is in him, very much to the purpose, this mistress, this absolute queen,

Reason, who by the effort she has it in herself to make, becomes perfect and becomes the supreme virtue. One must, to be truly a human being, give it full authority over that other part of the soul whose duty it is to obey the reason.

Cicero

*
* *

Be master of thy soul, O seeker of eternal verities, if thou wouldst attain thy end.

Book of Golden Precepts

Be master of thyself by taming thy heart, thy mind and thy senses; for each man is his own friend and his own enemy.

Mahabharata

Thy soul cannot be hurt in thee save by reason of thy ignorant body; direct and master them both.

Book of Golden Precepts

All things are lawful to me, but all things are not expedient; all things are lawful to me, but I will not be brought under the power of any.

I Corinthians

The Internal Law

The true law of life is so simple, clear and intelligible that men cannot excuse their bad living under the pretext of ignorance. If men live in contradiction to the law of their true living, they are repudiating reason. And that is in fact what they do.

Tolstoy

We should follow the law which Nature has engraved in our hearts. Wisdom lies in the perfect observation of her law.

Seneca

What is the true law? It is a right reason invariable, eternal, in conformity with Nature, which is extended in all human beings.

Cicero

Man's duty is to give the guidance of the soul to reason.

Hermes

The man whose understanding is in union with the Spirit, casts from him both good doing and evil doing; get this union, it is the perfect skill in works.

Bhagavad Gita

In verity, there exists one law only, the law of our conscience; all truth is there controlled and verified.

Antoine the Healer

Our conscience is an inner light which guides us with an infallible security, shows us everywhere the Good and invites us to cooperate in it; but the intelligence snatches it away from us under a veil whose stuff is of the imagination.

Antoine the Healer

The sovereign good has its abode in the soul; when that is upright, attentive to its duties, shut in upon itself, it has nothing to desire, it enjoys a perfect happiness.

Seneca

*
**

Learn what are the duties which are engraved in the hearts of men as their means of arriving to beatitude.

Laws of Manu

A one and single direction is needed which will conduct us to a one sole end.

Philo

Let the soul be submitted within to an upright judge whose authority extends over our most secret actions.

Seneca

Whosoever desireth salvation hath no expectation from man, but from him alone who dwelleth in him inwardly and from within the voice speaketh to him; then is he astonished that such words he hath never heard from any mouth, nor hath ever desired to hear them.

St. Barnabas

Quench not the spirit.

I Thessalonians

That which distinguishes from others the upright man, is that he never pollutes the genius within him which dwells in his heart.

Marcus Aurelius

If to thee nothing appears superior to the Genius which dwells in thee and has made itself master of his own tendencies and watches over his own thoughts and if beside him thou findest that all the rest is petty and of no worth, then to no other thing give lodging.

Marcus Aurelius

Neglect not the gift that is in thee.

I Timothy

Hearken unto thy soul in all thy works and be faithful unto it.

Ecclesiasticus

The soul is its own witness, the soul is its own refuge. Never despise thy soul, that supreme witness in men.

Laws of Manu

The Good Combat

Who has ruder battles to sustain than the man who labours for self-conquest?

Thomas à Kempis

He who subdues men is only strong; he who subdues himself, is mighty.

Lao Tse

Better is he that ruleth his spirit than he that taketh a city.

Proverbs

The greatest man in the world is not the conqueror, but the man who has domination over his own being.

Schopenhauer

A man may conquer thousands and thou-

sands of men in battle, but he is the greatest
conqueror who has mastered himself.

Fo-shu-hing-tsan-king

Self-conquest is the most glorious of victories;
it shall better serve a man to conquer himself than
to be master of the whole world.

Dhammapada

When a man has subdued himself and lives
in perfect continence, not god, not Gandharva, not
Mara, not Brahma himself can turn into defeat his
victory.

Dhammapada

*
**

All you have to do then is to command
yourselves.

Cicero

Keep over your actions an absolute empire;
be not their slave, but their master.

Thomas à Kempis

If you succeed in conquering yourself entirely, you will conquer the rest with the greatest ease. To triumph over oneself is the perfect victory.

Thomas à Kempis

He that overcometh shall inherit all things.

Revelations

Wouldst thou that the world should submit to thee? Be busy then to fortify thy soul without ceasing.

Omar Khayyam

Never be cowardly in the face of sin; say not to thyself, "I cannot do otherwise, I am habituated, I am weak." As long as thou livest, thou canst always strive against sin and conquer it, if not today, tomorrow, if not tomorrow, the day after, if not the day after, surely before thy death. But if from the beginning thou renounce the struggle, thou renouncest the fundamental sense of living.

Tolstoy

Behold thou hast instructed many and thou hast strengthened the weak hands, thy words have upholden him that was falling and thou hast strengthened the feeble knees; but now it is come upon thee and thou faintest, it toucheth thee and thou art troubled.

Job

Be strong and of a good courage.

Joshua

Let the Godhead within thee protect there a virile being, respect-worthy, a chief, a man self-disciplined.

Marcus Aurelius

Thyself vindicate thyself.

Seneca

Subject thyself to thee.

Bhagavad Gita

Control by thy divine self thy lower being.

Book of Golden Precepts

Battle with all thy force to cross the great torrent of desire.

Buddhist Text

Fight the good fight, lay hold on eternal life.

I Timothy

*
**

Warriors! we call ourselves warriors? But of what fashion of warriors, tell me then, are we? We battle, O disciple, that is why we are called warriors. Why do we battle, O Master? For lofty virtue, for high discernment, for sublime wisdom, — that is why we are called warriors.

Anguttara Nikaya

We wrestle not against flesh and blood, but against principalities, against powers, against the rulers of the darkness of the world, against spiritual wickedness in high places.

Ephesians

* * *

I strive not against the world, but it is the world which strives against me.

Buddhist Text

It is better to perish in the battle against evil than to be conquered by it and remain living.

Padhama Sutta

SECTION IV

THE VICTORY OF THE DIVINE

The Root of Evil

It is the Blessed One, the sole Being, thou sayest, who dwells in every soul: whence then come the misery and sorrow to which he is condemned by his presence in the heart of the soul of man?

Bhagavata Purana

The Eternal is in every man, but all men are not in the Eternal; there lies the cause of their suffering.

Ramakrishna

Sorrow is the daughter of evil.

Dhammapada

The perfection of evil is to be ignorant of the Divine.

Hermes

This is the noble way in regard to the origin of suffering; its origin is that thirst made up of egoistic desires which produces individual existence and which now here, now there hunts for its self-satisfaction, and such is the thirst of sensation, the thirst of existence, the thirst of domination and well-being.

Buddhist Text

The consciousness which is born of the battle of the sense-organs with their corresponding objects, man finds agreeable and takes pleasure in it; it is in that pleasure that this thirst takes its origin, is developed and becomes fixed and rooted. The sensations which are born of the senses, man finds agreeable and takes pleasure in them; it is in that pleasure that this thirst takes its origin, is developed and becomes fixed and rooted. The perception and the representation of the objects sensed by the senses, man finds agreeable and takes pleasure in them; it is in that pleasure that this thirst takes origin, is developed and becomes fixed and rooted.

Buddhist Text

It is in the foundation of our being that the conditions of existence have their root. It is from the foundation of our being that they start up and take form.

Buddhist Text

The action of man made of desire, dislike and illusion starts from his own being, in himself it has its source and, wherever it is found, must come to ripeness, and wherever his action comes to ripeness, man gathers its fruits whether in this or some other form of life.

Buddhist Text

Desire is the profoundest root of all evil; it is from desire that there has arisen the world of life and sorrow.

Pali Canon

Like burning coals are our desires; they are full of suffering, full of torment and a yet heavier distressfulness.

Buddhist Text

No living being possessed by desire can escape from sorrow. Those who have full understanding of this truth, conceive a hatred for desire.

Fo-shu-hing-tsan-king

The man who has conquered his unreined desires, offers no hold to sorrow; it glides over him like water over the leaves of the lotus.

Buddhist Text

They have sown the wind and they shall reap the whirlwind.

Hosea

Every action a man performs in thought, word and act, remains his veritable possession. It follows him and does not leave him even as a shadow separates not by a line from him who casts it.

Buddhist Text

The fruit of coveting and desire ripens in sorrow; pleasant at first it soon burns, as a torch burns the hand of the fool who has not in time cast it from him.

Sutra in Forty-two Articles

Such a fire, such an endless burning, that is Hell. It is not kindled by any devil, but it is within the heart that the mind incessantly lights, feeds and keeps it in being.

Gyokai

Hell has not been created by any one, but when a man does evil, he lights the fires of hell and burns in his own fire.

Mahommed

The essential spiritual being is so noble that even the damned cannot wish to cease from being. But sins form a partition and provoke so great a darkness and dissimilarity between the forces and the being in whom God lives that the spirit cannot unite itself to its own essence.

Ruysbroeck

If I regard myself as a martyr, I must think too of myself as that martyr's executioner; for we suffer only by the imagination of evil which is in us.

Antoine the Healer

The Healing

It is thus that for a very long time you have undergone suffering, affliction and distress and have augmented the harvests of death, long enough in very truth to have recognised suffering, long enough to have turned away from suffering, long enough to have enfranchised yourselves from suffering.

Sanyutta Nikaya

Return ye now every one from his evil way and make your ways and your doings good.

Jeremiah

Turn ye from your evil ways.

Ezekiel

Follow not a law of perdition, shut not yourselves up in negligence, follow not a law of falsehood; do nothing for the sake of the world.

Dhammapada

But now put off all these things.

Colossians

A man shall shake off every tie; for when he has no more attachment for form and name, when he is utterly without possessions, sorrow does not run after him.

Dhammapada

I know not anything, O my brothers, which so much gives birth to good, leads to the supreme happiness and destroys evil as vigilance, energy, moderation, contentment, wise reflection, a clear conscience, the friendship of the just, seeking after good and aversion from evil.

Anguttara Nikaya

Be ye holy in all manner of conduct.

I Peter

Though your sins be as scarlet, they shall be as white as snow.

Isaiah

Thou knowest, O my son, the way of regeneration.

Hermes

If thou art weary of suffering and affliction, do no longer any transgression, neither openly nor in secret.

Buddhist Text

Thou shalt heal thy soul and deliver it from all its pain and travailing.

Pythagoras

Do no evil and evil shall not come upon thee; be far from the unjust and sin shall be far from thee.

Ecclesiasticus

My son, give me thy heart and let thine eyes observe my ways.

Proverbs

Leave hereafter iniquity and accomplish righteousness.

Buddhist Text

Once thou hadst passions and namedst them evils. But now thou hast only virtues; they were born from thy passions. Thou broughtest into thy passions thy highest aim; then they became thy virtues and thy joys.

Nietzsche

Let all men accomplish only the works of righteousness, and they shall build for themselves a place of safety where they can store their treasures.

Buddhist Text

Let a man make haste towards good, let him turn away his thought from evil.

Dhammapada

The wise man sits not inert; he is ever

walking incessantly forward towards a greater light.

Fo-shu-hing-tsan-king

The good acts we do today, our own progress will show to us tomorrow as an evil, because we shall have acquired a greater light.

Antoine the Healer

The night is far spent, the day is at hand; let us therefore cast off the works of darkness and let us put on the armour of light.

Romans

Let us strive to destroy in ourselves all that is of the animal, that the humanity in us may be manifest.

Baha-ullah

Our creation, our perfection are our own work.

Antoine the Healer

To refrain from all evil, to speak always the truth, to abstain from all theft, to be pure and control the senses, that in sum constitutes the duty which the Manu has prescribed for the four classes.

Laws of Manu

In every way evil company should be abandoned, because it gives occasion to passion, wrath, folly, dissipation, loss of decision, loss of energy. These propensities are at first a bubbling froth, but they become as if oceans.

Narada Sutra

A man's spiritual gain depends on his ideas and sentiments; it is the product of his heart and not of his works.

Ramakrishna

For out of the heart proceed evil thoughts.

Matthew

One should, one can ameliorate one's life, not by external changes, but by a transformation of one's self in the soul. That one can do always and everywhere.

Tolstoy

Infected by the vices, the soul is swollen with poisons and can only be cured by knowledge and intelligence.

Hermes

For there is nothing so powerful to purify as knowledge.

Bhagavad Gita

The intelligence uncovers its light to the souls it governs and battles against their tendencies, even as a good physician uses fire and steel to combat the maladies of the body and recall it to health.

Hermes

When a man is delivered from all the dispositions of his heart which turn towards evil and not towards good and which can be extinguished, let him uproot them like the stock of a palm-tree, so that they shall be destroyed and have no power to sprout again. That I call a true repentance.

Mahavagga

The saintly disciple who applies himself in silence to right meditation, has surmounted covetousness, negligence, wrath, the inquietude of speculation and doubt; he contemplates and enlightens all beings friendly or hostile, with a limitless compassion, a limitless sympathy, a limitless serenity. He recognises that all internal phenomena are impermanent, subjected to sorrow and without substantial reality, and turning from these things he concentrates his mind on the permanent.

Buddhist Text

He should sanctify his soul, for it is there that there sits the eternal Beloved; he should deliver his mind from all that is the water and mire of things without reality, vain shadows, so as to keep in himself no trace of love or hatred; for love may lead into the evil way and hatred prevents us from following the good path.

Baha-ullah

Whosoever is truly enlightened, cannot fail to arrive at perfection.

Confucius

As the darkness of centuries is scattered when the light is brought into a chamber, so the accumulated faults of numberless births vanish before a single shaft of the light of the Almighty.

Ramakrishna

If iron is once changed to gold by the touch of the philosopher's stone, it may be kept in the earth or thrown into a mass of ordure, but always it will be gold and can never go back to its first condition. So is it with him whose heart has touched, were it but a single time, the feet of the Almighty; let him dwell amidst the tumult of the world or in the solitude of the forest, by nothing can he again be polluted.

Ramakrishna

Purification

Unto the pure all things are pure, but unto them that are defiled nothing is pure.

Titus

Blessed are the pure in heart.

Luke

Blessed is he who keepeth himself pure.

Koran

Happy is the man whose senses are purified and utterly under curb.

Udanavagga

His purity has brought him many profitable things, and this in the first rank, to know his soul.

Apollonius of Tyana

Purity is, next to birth, the greatest good that can be given to man.

Zend-Avesta

Step by step, piece by piece, hour by hour, the wise man should purify his soul of all impurity as a silver-worker purifies silver.

Dhammapada

By the practice of benevolence, tenderness, good will and indifference to the objects of happiness and sorrow, virtue and vice the mind arrives at its purification.

Patanjali

Whosoever purifies his own nature by holy thoughts, good words and good actions, has the real purity. Right nature is the true purification. In this visible world the true purification is for each man the right nature of his own natural being. And this nature is right in him when he purifies himself by holy thoughts, good words and good actions.

Zend-Avesta

Whosoever recognises at all times his faults of omission and cleanses himself by observing the ways of purity in each one of his actions, shall attain to perfection.

Udanavagga

To discern the eternal Reality and to detach oneself from the world are the two means of purification of the human heart.

Ramakrishna

The mind is a clear and polished mirror and our continual duty is to keep it pure and never allow dust to gather upon its face.

Zen Buddhist Saying

When a mirror is covered with dust, it cannot reflect the image cast upon it, it can only do that when it is without spot. It is so with beings. If their minds are not clear of stain, the Absolute cannot reveal himself in them; but if they free themselves from pollution, then shall he reveal himself within their being.

Ashwaghosha

The light of the sun is the same everywhere where it may fall, but it is the clear surfaces, water and mirror and polished metals, that can give its perfect reflection. Even such is the light of the Divine. It falls equally and impartially on every heart, but only the clean and pure heart can perfectly reflect it.

Ramakrishna

The soiled mirror reflects never the sunbeams, and the unclean and impure heart which is subjected to Maya, can never perceive the glory of the Eternal. But the pure in heart sees the Eternal, even as the clear mirror reflects the sun.

Ramakrishna

A torrent of clarity streams from the mind which is purified in full of all its impurities.

Buddhist Text

By the purity of the thoughts, of the actions, of holy words one cometh to know Ahura-Mazda.

Zend-Avesta

Blessed are the pure in heart, for they shall see God.

Matthew

Now we see through a glass darkly, but then face to face.

I Corinthians

Having therefore these promises, dearly beloved, let us cleanse ourselves from all pollution of the flesh and spirit.

II Corinthians

Be ye clean, ye that bear the vessels of the Lord.

Isaiah

Cleanse your hands, ye sinners, and purify your hearts, ye double minded.

James

Say in yourselves, "In the midst of this world of corruption, I would resemble the lotus which remains intangible by the mire in which it is born."

Sutra in Forty-two Articles

Thus strive by the faith of love to burn the veils of the demoniac nature over the soul that thou mayst purify thy mind and make it ready to understand.

Baha-ullah

Let thy mind be pure like gold, firm like a rock, transparent as crystal.

Angelus Silesius

Thou seekest after Paradise and thou longest to arrive where thou shalt be free from all sorrow and disunion; appease thy heart and make it white and pure, then art thou even here in Paradise.

Angelus Silesius

Knowest thou not that thou nurturest in

thyself a god? It is a god whom thou usest for thy strength, a god whom thou carriest with thee everywhere, and thou knowest it not at all, O unhappy man. And thinkest thou that I speak of a silver or golden idol outside thee? The god of whom I speak, thou carriest within thee and perceivest not that thou pollutest him by thy impure thoughts and infamous actions.

Epictetus

Purify thyself and thou shalt see God. Transform thy body into a temple, cast from thee evil thoughts and contemplate God with the eye of thy conscious soul.

Vamana

Renovate thyself daily.

Chinese Buddhist Inscription

The Great Choice

Four kinds of men have I found in the world, and what are the four? Men who are their own torturers, but cause no suffering to others; men who prepare suffering for others, but not for themselves; men who do evil both to themselves and to others; men who are the cause of pain neither to others nor to themselves. And I have found still four other kinds of men in the world, and what are the four? Men who think only of themselves and not of others; men who think of others and not of themselves; men who think of others as much as of themselves; men who think neither of themselves nor of others.

Anguttara Nikaya

And I have found still four other kinds of men in the world, and what are the four? Men who work only for their own deliverance and not for the deliverance of others; men who work for the deliverance of others and not for their own; men who work as much for their own deliverance as for the deliverance of others; men who care neither for others' deliverance nor for their own. And I have found yet four other kinds of men in the world, and what are the four? Men who instruct themselves without instructing others; men who instruct others without instructing themselves; men who instruct themselves in instructing others; men who instruct none, neither others nor themselves.

Anguttara Nikaya

And I have found still four other kinds of men in the world, and what are they? Men who do only the actions that are good; men who do only the actions that are evil; men who do actions that are in part good and in part evil; and men who do actions neither good nor evil, they who consecrate themselves to a work that leads to the cessation of works.

Anguttara Nikaya

Who really crosses over the Illusion? One who has renounced evil company, associates with men of noble mind, has put away the idea of property, frequents solitary places, tears himself away from the servitude of the world, transcends the qualities of Nature and abandons all anxiety for his existence, renounces the fruit of his works, renounces works, is freed from the dualities, renounces even the Vedas, and helps others to the passage, such is the one who crosses over the Illusion; he indeed traverses it and he helps others to pass.

Anguttara Nikaya

*
**

Ten knots of bondage: the illusion of personality; doubt; belief in the efficacy of rites and religious practices; sensuality; ill will; desire of a future life in the world of form; desire of a future life in the world of the formless; pride; unquietness; ignorance.

Narada Sutra

Ten high virtues: benevolence; spiritual life; intelligence; renunciation; perseverance; energy; patience; truthfulness; love for others; equality of soul.

Sangita Sutta

What is the root of evil? Greed, disliking and delusion are the root of evil. And what then are the roots of good? To be free from greed and disliking and delusion is the root of good.

Sangita Sutta

What are the roots of evil? Desire, disliking, ignorance. And what then are the roots of good? Liberation from desire, disliking and ignorance.

Majjhima Nikaya

Three roots of evil: desire, disliking and ignorance.

Buddhist Text

Three roads to good: knowledge, the spiritual life and the control of the mind.

Sangita Sutta

Three kinds of thirst: the thirst of sensation, of existence and of annihilation.

Sangita Sutta

The contemplation of the impermanence of things, that wonderful gateway to Truth, leads us to victory over the thirst for the satisfaction of our desires.

Sangita Sutta

Whether on earth or in the abodes of the gods, all beings are upon three evil paths; they are in the power of existence, desire and ignorance.

Lalita Vistara

But the fruit of the spirit is love, joy, peace, long-suffering, gentleness, goodness, faith, meekness, temperance.

Lalita Vistara

By righteousness is the way to a higher region, but by unrighteousness to a lower region; by knowledge cometh freedom, but by ignorance the prolongation of bondage.

Galatians

What are the four mighty combats? The battle to keep from waking the evil which yet is not; the battle to repel the evil that is already in existence; the battle to awaken the good which yet is not; the battle to preserve and develop the good that is already in existence.

Sankhya Karika

Four roads to perfection: the way of the novice, the way of the warrior, the way of the conqueror, the way of the saint. Four conditions that we may enter into the way: the society of the just, an ear given to instruction, vigilance, a life of righteousness.

Anguttara Nikaya

*
**

Two kinds of joy are there, O my brothers, and what are they? The noisy and the silent joy; but nobler is the joy that is silent.

Sangita Sutta

Two kinds of joy are there, O my brothers,

and what are they? The joy of distraction and the joy of vigilance; but nobler is the joy that is heedful.

Buddhist Text

Two kinds of joy are there, O my brothers, and what are they? The joy of the sated senses and the joy of the equal soul; but nobler is the joy of equality.

Buddhist Text

Two kinds of joy are there, O my brothers, and what are they? The joy of the senses and the joy of the spirit; but nobler is the joy of the spirit.

Buddhist Text

Two kinds of joy are there, O my brothers, and what are they? The joy to possess and the joy to renounce; but nobler is the joy of renunciation.

Buddhist Text

Two kinds of joy are there, O my brothers,

and what are they? The joy of egoism and the joy to forget oneself; but nobler is the joy of self-oblivion.

Buddhist Text

*
**

There is an internal war in man between reason and the passions. He could get some peace if he had only reason without passions or only passions without reason, but because he has both, he must be at war, since he cannot have peace with one without being at war with the other. Thus he is always divided and in opposition to himself.

Pascal

For the good that I would do, I do not; but the evil that I would not, that I do. . . . I find then a law that, when I would do good, evil is present with me.

Romans

I approve the better way, but I follow the worse.

Horace

We have the choice; it depends on us to choose the good or the evil by our own will. The choice of evil draws us to our physical nature and subjects us to fate.

Hermes

The union of the soul and nature has for its only object to give the soul the knowledge of nature and make it capable of eternal freedom.

Sankhya Karika

*
**

No man can serve two masters.

Matthew

It is not possible, O my son, to be attached at once to perishable things and to things divine; the one or the other one must choose, one cannot cling to both at once.

Hermes

Endeavour maketh wisdom to grow, but

negligence increaseth perdition. Perceive the double way of descent and ascension and choose the way that increaseth wisdom.

Dhammapada

Behold, there is the goal of beatitude and there the long road of suffering. Thou canst choose the one or the other across the cycles to come.

Book of Golden Precepts

I have chosen the way of truth.

Psalms

I would follow the road of straightness, the unstained way of which the sages speak, which has no windings and leads straight to deliverance.

Buddhist Text

One road conducts to the goods of this world, honour and riches, but the other to victory over the world. Seek not the goods of the world,

riches and honour. Let your aim be to transcend
the world.

Buddhist Text

Enter ye in at the strait gate: for wide is
the gate and broad is the way that leadeth to
destruction.

Luke

Walk in the spirit, and ye shall not fulfil the
lust of the flesh; — for the flesh lusteth against the
spirit and the desire of the spirit is against the
flesh; and these are contrary the one to the other.

Galatians

O friends, despise not the eternal Beauty for
the mortal beauty, and be not held back by the
things of the earth.

Baha-ullah

You shall wander in the darkness and see not
till you have found the eternal Light.

Dhammapada

Aspire to the regions where oneness has its dominion.

Fo-shu-hing-tsan-king

Beyond fugitive Time reigns in the silence the kingdom of the Permanent. O happy he who conquers here and penetrates into the country of peace!

Udanavagga

To Choose Today

Now it is high time to awake out of sleep.... The night is far spent, the day is at hand; let us therefore cast off the works of darkness and put on the armour of light.

Romans

One says, when my son Harish shall have grown up, I will marry him off, give up the burden of the family, renounce the world and begin to practise Yoga. To him the Lord replies: You will never find the opportune moment to practise Yoga; for you will then say, 'Harish and Girish are very fond of me and cannot do without me', you will no doubt desire that Harish should have a son and the son marry. There will never be an end to your desires.

Ramakrishna

The world is an eternal present, and the present is now; what was is no more and who can say what will come or whether tomorrow morning the dawn will arise.

Anaximander

This is why I would put to profit the present moment, penetrated with the conviction that now has come the right moment to seek for the Truth.

Fo-shu-hing-tsan-king

It is easier today to triumph over evil habits than it will be tomorrow.

Confucius

The present is the most precious moment. Use all the forces of thy spirit not to let that moment escape thee.

Tolstoy

Let not the favourable moment pass thee by, for those who have suffered it to escape them, shall lament when they find themselves on the path which leads to the abyss.

Buddhist Text

How shouldst thou not profit by thy age of strength to issue from the evil terrain?

Kin-yuan-li-sao

How then shalt thou discover in thy age what in thy youth thou hast not gathered in?

Ecclesiasticus

Seek out swiftly the way of righteousness; turn without delay from that which defiles thee.

Buddhist Text

Knowest thou not that thy life, whether long or brief, consists only of a few breathings?

Farid-uddin Attar

Enter not into questions of the vicissitudes of this world, ask not of things to come. Regard as booty won the present moment; trouble not thyself with the past, question not of the future.

Omar Khayyam

Thou hast lost thyself in the search for the mystery of life and death; but seek out thy path before thy life be taken from thee. If living thou find it not, hopest thou to reach this great mystery when thou art dead?

Farid-uddin Attar

If today when thou art with thy self, thou knowest nothing, what wilt thou know tomorrow when thou shalt have passed out of this self?

Omar Khayyam

Thou canst create this day thy chances for tomorrow. In this great journey the causes thou sowest in every hour bear each its harvest of results.

Book of Golden Precepts

One life, one flash of time between two eternities. No second chance for us, — no, never. It will be well for us if we can live like sages in the utter reality.

Anonymous

Life or Death

See, I have set before thee this day life and good, and death and evil.

Deuteronomy

Life is like a moth which in summer at nightfall turns about a lamp; there it finds at first a fugitive joy, but afterwards death.

Zeisho Aishako

When lust hath conceived, it bringeth forth sin; and sin, when it is finished, bringeth forth death.

James

For the wages of sin is death.

Romans

Sin is nothing other than man's act of turning

his face away from God and himself towards death.

Angelus Silesius

The wicked have called unto them death by their works and their words; they have taken death for their friend and have been consumed, they have made alliance with him, because of such companionship they were worthy.

Wisdom

There is a way that seemeth right unto a man, but the end thereof are the ways of death.

Proverbs

In the way of righteousness is life: and in the pathway thereof there is no death.

Proverbs

As righteousness tendeth to life, so he that pursueth evil, pursueth it to his own death.

Proverbs

Heedlessness is the road of death.

Buddhist Text

To be heedful of one's soul is the way to immortality, but heedlessness is the highway of death. They who persevere and are heedful shall not perish, but the careless are even now as if souls that are dead.

Dhammupada

The man that wandereth out of the way of understanding, shall remain in the congregation of the dead.

Proverbs

That man whose mind attaches itself only to sensible objects, death carries away like a torrent dragging with it a sleeping village.

Dhammapada

Whatsoever a man soweth, that shall he also reap. He that soweth to his flesh, shall reap corruption: but he that soweth to the Spirit, shall of the Spirit reap life everlasting.

Galatians

For they that are after the flesh, do mind the things of the flesh, but they that are after the Spirit, the things of the Spirit. To be carnally minded is death, to be spiritually minded is life and peace.

Romans

Whosoever has come to know himself, has come to the perfect good; but he who by an error of love has set his love on the body, remains lost in darkness and subjected by his senses to the conditions of death.

Hermes

The foolish follow after the desires that are outward and they fall into the snare of death that is wide open for them, but the wise man sets his mind on the immortal and the certain and longs not here below for uncertain and transient things.

Katha Upanishad

When all the desires that trouble the heart have fallen silent, then this mortal puts on immortality.

Katha Upanishad

**

By the understanding of the impermanence, of subjection to grief and of the unreality of substance of all formations arises the light of the true wisdom and without it there can be no veritable illumination. The gate of the Way is found in this understanding. Whoever strives not to come to it, is torn into pieces by death.

Fo-shu-hing-tsan-king

Who goeth into the next world undelivered from death, even as here death respecteth nothing, so in that world too shall he be its perpetual prey.

Shatapatha Brahmana

The way of life is above to the wise that he may depart from hell which is beneath.

Proverbs

When the wicked turneth away from his wickedness and doeth that which is lawful and right, he shall save his soul alive. Because he considereth and turneth away from all his transgressions that he hath committed, he shall surely live, he shall not die.

Ezekiel

The pure shall not die, but he who leads not the spiritual life dies without ceasing. The wise man knows this difference and takes pleasure in purity and spirituality; it is his joy to live like the saints.

Udanavagga

When one follows the Way, there is no death upon the earth.

Lao Tse

Death is swallowed up in victory.

I Corinthians

When this corruptible shall have put on incorruption and this mortal shall have put on immortality, then shall be brought to pass the saying that is written, "Death is swallowed up in victory."

I Corinthians

The last enemy that shall be destroyed is death.

I Corinthians

*
**

Why, O men born from the earth, do you yield yourselves to death, when it is permitted to you to obtain immortality? Return to yourselves, O you who walk in error and languish in ignorance, withdraw from the light that is darkness, renounce corruption, take part in immortality.

Hermes

Cease to search out death with such ardour in the strayings of your life, use not the work of your hands to win that which shall destroy you.

Wisdom

Forsake your ignorance and live.

Proverbs

If ye live after the flesh, ye shall die; but if ye through the Spirit do mortify the deeds of the body, ye shall live.

Romans

For this corruptible must put on incorruption and this mortal must put on immortality.

I Corinthians

*
**

Take me from non-being to being, take me from death to immortality. The non-being, it is death; but the being is the immortal. From death take me to that which dies not, let me be that which is immortal.

Brihadaranyaka Upanishad

O mortal, the enchantress sensuality is dragging thee like an untameable horse to the bottom of the tomb. Death will suddenly give the rein to thy courser and thou shalt not avail to hold her back from the fatal descent.

Saadi

Be not taken in the snares of the Prince of death, let him not cast thee to the ground because thou hast been heedless.

Buddhist Text

I know thy works, that thou hast a name that thou livest, and art dead.

Revelations

Depart from evil and do good; and dwell for evermore.

Psalms

Above all thou must tear this robe that thou wearest, this garment of ignorance which is the principle of wickedness, this dark covering, this

living death, this tomb which thou carriest about
with thee.

Hermes

W hen thy soils shall have vanished and thou
art free of defect, thou shalt no more be subject to
decay and death.

Dhammapada

W hen thou art purified of thy omissions and
thy pollutions, thou shalt come by that which is
beyond age and death.

Buddhist Text

S trive forcefully, cross the current.

Dhammapada

C ross forcefully the torrent flood of the
world.

Dhammapada

To it with good heart, O pilgrim, on to that other shore!

Book of Golden Precepts

Few among men come to that other shore of deliverance; the common run of mortals only wander parallel to its bank. But those who are consecrated to Truth and live according to its Law and strive for only one end, they shall come by that other shore and they shall swim across death's impetuous torrent.

Dhammapada

Those who are consecrated to Truth shall surely gain the other shore and they shall cross the torrent waves of death.

Buddhist Text

The Second Birth

To transform death and make of it a means of victory and triumph.

Nietzsche

What use to cut the branches if one leaves the roots?

Apollonius of Tyana

Death is the only remedy against death.

Farid-uddin Attar

There is one only way of salvation, to renounce the life which perishes and to live the life in which there is no death.

Tolstoy

To know how to die in one age gives us life in all the others.

Giordano Bruno

To surmount this thirst of existence, to reject it, to be liberated from it, to give it no farther harbourage.

Mahavagga

He that loveth his life, shall lose it; and he that hateth his life in this world, shall keep it unto life eternal.

John

The sage does not die any more, for he is already dead, dead to all vanity, dead to all that is not God.

Angelus Silesius

He is in truth the man of piety who is dead even in his lifetime, that is to say, whose passions and desires have been destroyed and are like a body that is dead.

Ramakrishna

Those I love who know how to live only to disappear, for they pass beyond.

Nietzsche

*
**

None can be saved without being reborn.

Hermes

He who conceives the Truth, is born anew.

Vamana

The splendour which inundates all his thought and all his soul, snatches him from the ties of the body and transforms his whole being into the very essence of God.

Hermes

Whosoever comes to birth in God, is delivered from the physical sensations, recognises the different elements which compose it and enjoys a perfect happiness.

Hermes

That is the supreme felicity of those who have won their victory, it is the perfect and immutable peace, the defeat of Impermanence, a pure and luminous condition, the victory over death.

Pali Canon

**
*

So long as we do not die to ourselves and are not indifferent to creatures, the soul will not be free.

Farid-uddin Attar

How shall we conquer the old man in us? When the flower becomes a fruit, the petals fall of themselves; so when the divinity increases in us, all the weaknesses of human nature vanish of their own accord.

Ramakrishna

The ideal birth is perfected, the twelfth executioner is driven forth and we are born to contemplation.

Hermes

Old things are passed away, behold all things are become new.

II Corinthians

I have issued out of myself, I have put on an immortal body, I am no longer the same, I am born into wisdom.

Hermes

Now this is the counsel which I give to kings and Churches and to all that has grown weak by age and virtue, "Allow yourselves to be overthrown that you may recover life and the virtue return to you."

Nietzsche

Before the creator can be born, there must be many pangs and transformations. Yes, your life must pass through many bitter deaths, O creators.

Nietzsche

Ye must be born again.

John

Purge out therefore the old leaven, that ye may be a new lump.

I Corinthians

And be not conformed to this world, but be ye transformed by the renewing of your mind.

Romans

Ye have been taught that ye put off the old man which is corrupt according to the deceitful lusts and be renewed in the spirit of your mind, that ye put on the new man.

Ephesians

Repent and be converted.

Acts of the Apostles

Return and turn back from all your transgressions that your iniquity be not your ruin. Cast from you all the transgressions which you have committed and make yourselves a new heart and a new mind.

Ezekiel

For you were sometimes darkness, but now are light; walk as children of light.

Ephesians

You shall no more carry in yourselves the root of evil; disease and infirmity no more shall make war against you and corruption shall flee from you for ever into oblivion.

Esdras

*
**

That which is born of the flesh, is flesh, and that which is born of the Spirit, is spirit. Marvel not that I said unto thee, "Ye must be born again."

John

Awake thou that sleepest and arise from the dead.

Ephesians

Renew thyself utterly day by day; make thyself new and again new and ever again new.

Tseng Tse

Despair not, my son, thy desire shall be fulfilled, thy will shall have fruit; put to sleep the sensations of the body and thou shalt be born in God.

Hermes

It is then alone that thou canst become one who walks in heaven, one of those who walk on the winds and above the waves and their feet shall not touch the waters.

Book of Golden Precepts

So long as thou art not dead to all things, one by one, thou canst not set thy feet in this portico.

Farid-uddin Attar

Thou must pass over thyself to mount beyond, ever higher till the stars themselves are below thee.

Nietzsche

O sage, very high raise thyself, even to the most high dwelling of Truth.

Mahavagga

Since the world passes, thyself pass beyond it.

Farid-uddin Attar

The Perfect Union

There are the veils torn which distinguish from each other these manifestations and he will soar up from the world of the passions to the heaven of the One.

Baha-ullah

There are no partitions between ourselves and the Infinite.

Emerson

Men who are sovereignly perfect resemble the earth by the greatness and depth of their wisdom, the heavens by its height and splendour, Space and illimitable Time by its extent and duration.

Tsu Tse

As for those who have risen more high, they make no distinction between cause and effect, and those who, higher still in the eternal cities, dwell in the flowering gardens, know not cause nor effect, both are to them absolutely foreign, for, rapid as the lightning, they have passed the kingdom of Names and qualities and they dwell with the divine Essence.

Baha-ullah

The One is attained when man arrives at ripeness in one of these three states of his spirit, "All is myself," "All is thou," "Thou art the Master, I the servant."

Ramakrishna

To Him when the sages come, they are satisfied in knowledge, desire passes away from them, they have perfected the self, they enter in on every side into the All who pervades all things and they are united with him for ever.

Mundaka Upanishad

This evolution lasts until we reach the absolute purity of the Being. Then we arrive at divinity. We form a vast oneness. We enjoy an entirety of divine power; we are united in a single love; we are God.

Antoine the Healer

*
**

The soul which has reached this state, loses itself and is submerged in the deep sea of Divinity, so that it can say, "God is within me, God is outside me, God is everywhere around me, he replaces all things for me and I know Him only and nothing else."

Tauler

The saint who has arrived at a perfect contemplation, sees the All as one only spirit and his soul loses itself in this spirit, as water is dissolved in water, as fire is united to fire, as air is made one with air.

Shankaracharya

He sees the one Spirit in all beings and he sees all beings in the one Spirit.

Bhagavad Gita

Thus seeing the supreme Spirit equally in all beings and all beings in the supreme Spirit, he, offering his soul in sacrifice, identifies himself with the Being who shines in his own splendour.

Manu

Knowing the elements, knowing the worlds, knowing all the regions and the spaces, adoring the first-born Word, understanding heaven, earth and air to be only He, knowing that the worlds, discovering that Space and the solar orb are He alone, he sees this supreme Being, he becomes that Being, he is identified in union with Him and completes this vast and fertile web of solemn sacrifice.

Sarvamedha Upanishad

Then, accomplished in knowledge, he shakes from him good and evil, and stainless, reaches that supreme Equality.

Mundaka Upanishad

As the rivers flow into the ocean and lose their name and form, the sage losing name and form disappears into the supreme Spirit and himself becomes that Spirit.

Mundaka Upanishad

As the floods when they have thrown themselves into the ocean, lose their name and their form and one cannot say of them, "Behold, they are here, they are there," though still they are, so one cannot say of the Perfect when he has entered into the supreme Nirvana, "He is here, he is there," though he is still in existence.

Buddhist Meditation

The traveller in this valley may seem to be seated in the dust, but in truth he sits upon spiritual heights receiving the eternal favours, drinking the exquisite wine of the spirit.

Baha-ullah

He feels himself to be master of the universe, his "I" floats in power above this gulf and will range across eternity above these infinite vicissitudes. His spirit endeavours to announce and spread harmony. And through endless ages his union with Self and his creation which surrounds him will increase in perfection.

Novalis

*
**

Such is the last good of those who possess knowledge: to become God.

Hermes

The soul bound is man; free, it is God.

Ramakrishna

Dost thou not know that thou hast become God and art the son of the One?

Hermes

The Perfect Peace

If a man possesses the true light, darkness cannot lodge in his soul. Who can describe the peace of that luminous country where the true light shines out for ever in its limpid purity?

Thomas à Kempis

The happiness of each thing resides in its own proper perfection, and this perfection is nothing else for each individual than union with its own Cause.

Sallust

The man in whose vision all things are becomings of the Self and who sees in all things oneness, whence shall he have grief or delusion?

Isha Upanishad

The sage having perceived God by the spiritual union casts from him grief and joy.

Katha Upanishad

Who in the world of plurality sees the One Existence and in the world of shadows seizes this Reality, to him belongs the eternal peace, to none else, to none else.

Vivekananda

The one controlling inner Self of all existences who makes his one form into many kinds of form, him the sages see in themselves; theirs is the eternal peace and it is not for others.

Katha Upanishad

The sages who see the eternal in things transient, for them is the peace eternal.

Katha Upanishad

*
**

In mosque and church and synagogue one has the terror of hell and the seeking for Paradise, but the seed of that disquiet has never sprouted in the heart which has entered into the secrets of the Almighty.

Omar Khayyam

When man has seen that he is one with the infinite being of the universe, all separation is at an end, all men, women, angels, gods, animals, plants, the whole world lost in this oneness, then all fear disappears.

Vivekananda

When one perceives clearly this Self as God and as the Lord of all that is and will be, he knows no longer any fear.

Brihadaranyaka Upanishad

When one knows God without beginning and end in the midst of the complex mass of things, the creator of all who takes many forms, the One who envelops the universe, he is delivered from all bondage.

Shwetashwatara Upanishad

Good and evil cannot bind him who has realised the oneness of nature and self with the Eternal.

Ramakrishna

When he knows that he is That, the Eternal, he is delivered from all limitations.

Raivatya Upanishad

The traveller in the valley of knowledge who sees the end of each thing, knows how to find peace amid contest and reconciliation amidst disunion.

Baha-ullah

To him justice and injustice are equal, knowledge and ignorance have the same value, for he has broken the cage of personality and desire and he has flown on the wings of immortality towards the eternal heavens.

Baha-ullah

In this state he will submit to destiny, making no more of disorder than of order. Death gives him a comprehension of immortality; he sees with the spiritual eye the mystery of resurrection in men and things and his heart makes him feel the divine wisdom in these infinite manifestations.

Baha-ullah

He whose whole play of life is with the Self and in the Self has his joy and so does actions, is the best of the knowers of the Eternal.

Mundaka Upanishad

Void of wishes, controlled in mind and spirit, abandoning all desire of external possession, satisfied with what comes to him, free from liking and disliking and from all jealousy and envy, equal in success and failure, he acts and is not bound by his actions.

Bhagavad Gita

As a bird of the waters, such as the pelican, can dive into the waves and his plumage is not wetted, the liberated soul lives in the world, but is not affected by the world.

Ramakrishna

When the soul attains to its divine estate, it can live in constant contact with innumerable unregenerated souls without being affected by the contact.

Ramakrishna

The present world and the next are but a drop of water whose existence is of no account.

Farid-uddin Attar

If we drink of this cup, we shall forget the whole world.

Baha-ullah

The lines are fallen to me in pleasant places; yea, I have a goodly heritage.... Therefore my heart is glad and my spirit rejoiceth; my flesh also shall rest in security.

Psalms

The Perfect Knowledge

The veils that hide the light shall be rent asunder.

Baha-ullah

The soul when it has arrived at unity, acquires a supernatural knowledge.

Lao Tse

All Nature will be transfigured to them and the book of knowledge lie open. They will not need to have recourse to books in order to know; their own thought will have become their book and will contain an infinite knowledge.

Vivekananda

When the spark of truth is discovered in the spirit, all is taught to it that it needs.

Ruysbroeck

The virtue of a man who has attained to the

height of perfection, extends even to a fore-knowledge of the future.

Confucius

When the mind is one with the deeper spirit and wholly in touch with knowledge, its universality embraces all things.

Patanjali

When the mind is one with the deeper spirit, there results the absolute knowledge of the self.

Patanjali

That man who is without darkness, exempt from evil, absolutely pure, although of all things which are in the world of the ten regions since unbeginning time till today, he knows none, has seen none, has heard of none, has not in a word any knowledge of them however small, yet has he the high knowledge of omniscience. It is in speaking of him that one can use the word enlightenment.

Sutra in Forty-two Articles

The man who has plunged deep into a pure knowledge of the profound secrets of the spirit, is neither a terrestrial nor a celestial being. He is the most high spirit robed in the perishable body, the sublime and very Divinity.

Pico della Mirandola

His faculties are so ample, so vast, so profound that it is as if an immense source from which everything issues in its time. They are as vast and extended as the heavens; the hidden source from which they issue is deep as the abyss.

Tsu Tse

And then lost in the Eternal, he is luminous, he is without body and matter, he is pure, he is delivered from all suffering and stain, he knows, he foresees, he masters everything, and beings appear to him what they were from eternity, constantly like unto themselves.

Isha Upanishad

*
**

The seeker will discover himself with new

eyes, a new understanding, a new heart and a new soul, and with them he shall see the evident signs of the world and the obscure secrets of the soul, and he will understand that in the least object there is found a door by which one enters into the domain of self-evidence, certitude and conviction.

Baha-ullah

Each moment, each hour will bring him the vision of a new mystery, because his heart is detached from this as from the other world; an invisible aid guides all his steps and fires his ardour.

Baha-ullah

In each thing he will see the mystery of the transfiguration and the divine apparition.

Baha-ullah

At each instant he sees a wonderful world and a new creation.

Baha-ullah

When his mind shall be enfranchised from human things, then shall he enter into the city of marvellous wisdom which ever renews itself and grows in beauty from age to age.

Baha-ullah

He shall contemplate under the veil millions of secrets as radiant as the sun.

Farid-uddin Attar

He will see with the divine eyes the mysteries of the eternal art.

Baha-ullah

Some men only have the happiness to raise themselves to that perception of the Divine which exists only in God and in the human mind.

Hermes

Thou who by the force of thy heroism hast reached the unlimited exercise of a divine intelligence, thou hast wisdom for the force of thy means and gentleness for the force of thy pure action.

Lalita Vistara

Reflect attentively with all thy knowledge on the divine manifestation in all things of a glorious unity; purify thy understanding from the sentences of men that thou mayst hear the sacred and divine harmonies which come from all directions; sanctify thy heart from all the superstitions of the past that thou mayst understand the simple, direct and marvellous Revelation.

Baha-ullah

And before thee she shall open wide the portals of her secret chambers and under thy eyes she shall lay bare the treasures hidden in the deeps of her bosom. But she shows not her treasures save to the eye of the spirit, the eye which is never closed, the eye which is met by no veil in any of the kingdoms of her empire.

Book of Golden Precepts

It is then that she shall show to thee the

means and the way, the first and the second and the third even to the seventh door. Last the end, beyond which are extended and bathed in light of the spiritual sun glories inexpressible and invisible to all save only to the soul's eye.

Book of Golden Precepts

Thou shalt hear what no ear has heard, thou shalt see what no eye has seen.

Ahmed Halif

And at last thou shalt come into that place where thou shalt find only one sole being in place of the world and its mortal creatures.

Ahmed Halif

That man, O beloved, who knows this imperishable Spirit in which the Self is gathered with all its powers, lives and creatures, penetrates into all things and becomes omniscient.

Prashna Upanishad

Equal in heart, equal in thought thou hast won for thyself omniscience.

Lalita Vistara

Pass; thou hast the key, thou canst be at ease.

Book of Golden Precepts

Peace to him who has finished this supreme journey under the guidance of the Truth and the Light!

Baha-ullah

We have known thee, O most great Light who art perceived only by the intelligence! We have known thee, O Plenitude, matrix of all Nature! We have known thee, O eternal Permanence!

Hermes

BOOK THREE

THE UNION OF ALL IN THE ONE IN ALL

SECTION I

DEATH AND IMMORTALITY

Death

Dust thou art and unto dust shalt thou return.

Genesis

The days of our years are threescore years and ten, and if by reason of strength they be fourscore years, yet is their strength labour and sorrow.

Psalms

Young and old and those who are growing to age, shall all die one after the other like fruits that fall.

Buddhist Text

Man falls not suddenly into death, but moves to meet him step by step. We are dying each day; each day robs us of a part of our existence.

Seneca

For what is our life! It is even a vapour that

appeareth for a little time and then vanisheth away.

James

Regard behind thee the abyss of duration and in front that other infinity of the ages to come. What difference is there in this immensity between one who has lived three days and one who has lived three human ages?

Marcus Aurelius

As a ripe fruit is at every moment in peril of detaching itself from the branch, so every creature born lives under a perpetual menace of death.

Buddhist Text

The lives of mortal men are like vases of many colours made by the potter's hands; they are broken into a thousand pieces; there is one end for all.

Buddhist Text

As the herdsman urges with his staff his

cattle to the stall, so age and death drive before them the lives of men.

Udanavagga

Like the waves of a river that flow slowly on and return never back, the days of human life pass and come not back again.

Buddhist Text

Like the waves of a rivulet, day and night are flowing through the hours of life and coming nearer and nearer to their end.

Buddhist Text

Time is a flood, an impetuous torrent which drags with it all that is born. A thing has scarcely appeared when it is carried away; another has already passed; and this other will soon fall into the gulf.

Marcus Aurelius

Nature wills that each thing after its fulfilment shall disappear; it is for this that everything ages and dies.

Apollonius of Tyana

Nothing is fixed, nothing stable, nothing immobile in nature, nor in heaven, nor on the earth.

Hermes

Nothing is wholly dead nor wholly alive.

Victor Hugo

It is at all times a sensible consolation to be able to say, "Death is as natural as life."

Schopenhauer

Death and decrepitude are inherent in the world. The sage who knows the nature of things, does not grieve.

Metta Sutta

Each thing in the world shoots out, flowers

and returns to its root. This return is in conformity with nature; therefore the destruction of the body is no danger to the being.

Lao Tse

Man when he dies, knows that nothing peculiar will happen to him, only what has already happened to millions of beings, and all he does is to change his mode of journeying, but it is impossible for him not to feel an emotion when he comes to the place where he must undergo the change.

Tolstoy

The dying man understands with difficulty what lives, not because his mental faculties are dulled, but because he understands something the living do not and cannot understand, and in this he is entirely absorbed.

Tolstoy

Death will work in me this transformation, that I shall pass into another being otherwise separated from the world. And then the whole world, while yet the same for those who live in it, will become other for me.

Tolstoy

When the present dream of our life is finished, a new dream will succeed it and there our life and death will not be known.

Schopenhauer

For things and their revolutions are like the images of a dream.... So long as the dream lasts, all this world appears real to us; the world exists no longer when the dream is finished.

Shankaracharya

All the earth is no more than a great tomb and there is nothing on its surface which is not hidden in the tomb, under earth.... All are hastening to bury themselves in the depths of the ocean of infinity. But be of good courage.... The sun is cradled in darkness and the need of the night is to reveal the splendour of the stars.

Totaku-ko-Nozagual

Immortality

Here have we no continuing city, but we seek one to come.

Hebrews

Though our outward man perish, yet the inward man is renewed day by day.

II Corinthians

That which we are is that, yes, it is that that we become, and if one knows it not, great is the perdition: it is they who have discovered it that become immortal.

Brihadaranyaka Upanishad

They rest from their labours and their works follow them.

Revelations

The deeds a man has accomplished follow

him in his journeying when he fares to another world.

Mahabharata

*
**

The voice which tells us that we are immortal is the voice of God within us.

Pascal

There are some who see by contemplation the self in themselves by the self, others by union through the understanding and others again know not, but hear of it from others and seek after it, and all these, even they who hear and seek after it, pass over beyond death.

Bhagavad Gita

Let him in whom there is understanding know that he is immortal.

Hermes

Those become immortal who know by the

heart and the understanding Him who in the heart has his dwelling-place.

Shwetashwatara Upanishad

When man has known beyond this world the Being who is hidden according to the form in every creature, the Lord who contains in himself all things, then he becomes immortal.

Shwetashwatara Upanishad

He who sees all things in the self and the self in all things, has doubt no longer.

Isha Upanishad

The sage having seen the Self in everything, when he leaves this world, becomes immortal.

Kena Upanishad

That being known which is without sound, touch or form, inexhaustible, eternal, without beginning or end, greater than the great self, immutable, man escapes from the mouth of death.

Katha Upanishad

He who thus knows, "I am the Eternal", the gods themselves cannot make him other, for he is their own self.

Brihadaranyaka Upanishad

Therefore neither you, O judges, nor men in general ought to fear death: they have only to remember one thing, that for a just man there is no ill in life and no ill in death.

Socrates

For the saint there is no death.

Tolstoy

Here is a man to whom all others are not-self: at bottom his own personality alone is real to him, the others in truth only phantasms: he recognises an existence in them, but it is relative, they can serve him as instruments of his designs or can come in his way and that is all: in short between his own personality and all of them there is a deep gulf, an immense distance. Look upon this man confronted by death: it seems to him as if with him all reality, the whole world were disappearing. Then look upon this other who recognises in all that are his like, more, in all that lives, himself, his own essence: he casts his existence into the existence of all living beings and by death he loses only a feeble portion of that existence, for he subsists in all the others in whom he has always recognised, has always loved his own being, his own essence, and it is only the illusion that is now about to fall away from him, the illusion which separated his consciousness from all others.

Schopenhauer

The Eternity of Beings

He who has a mistaken idea of life, will always have a mistaken idea of death.

Tolstoy

He who looks on the forms of existence as a form or a mirage, shall not see death.

Sanyutta Nikaya

He who regards the body as a mirage or as a flake of foam on the waves, shall no longer see death.

Dhammapada

In death he sees life.

Baha-ullah

The individual dies, the kind is indestructible. The individual is the expression in time of the kind which is outside time.

Schopenhauer

Men perish because they cannot join the beginning and the end.

Alcmaeon

All existences are unmanifest in their origin and beginning, manifest in their middle and unmanifest again in their passing; what cause is here to lament?

Bhagavad Gita

The soul that dwells in the body of every man is unslayable, and therefore thou shouldst not weep for all these beings.

Bhagavad Gita

The wise weep not for the dead nor the living: all of us were before and shall not cease to be hereafter.

Bhagavad Gita

There is no death, the word mortal has no

significance; death would be destruction and nothing is destroyed in the universe.

Hermes

                    *
                   **

The destruction of things is their return to the cause that has produced them.

Sankhya Pravachana

The origin of things is the Infinite: necessarily they disappear into that which put them into birth.

Anaximander

I will say more: there is no birth of terrestrial things and there is no disappearance of them by death's destruction, but only a reunion and a separation of materials assembled together: birth is only a word habitual to the human mind.

Empedocles

None dies except in appearance. In fact what is called birth is the passage from essence to substance, and what is called death is on the contrary the passage from substance to essence. Nothing is born and nothing dies in reality, but all first appears and then becomes invisible. The first effect is produced by the density of matter, the second by the subtlety of essence which remains always the same but is sometimes in movement, sometimes in repose.

Apollonius of Tyana

Nothing dies, but what was composed is divided: this division is not a death, it is the analysis of a combination; but the aim of this analysis is not destruction, it is a renewal.

Hermes

Life begins a long series of transformations, manifesting itself under innumerable forms, fashioning for itself in the sequence of the ages a multitude of transitory but ever more perfect organisms, thus perfecting itself by the progress of its faculties.

Antoine the Healer

P erfection is the end and the beginning of all things, and without perfection they could not be.

Confucius

**

T here is an eternal Thinker, but his thoughts are not eternal.

Katha Upanishad

A ll that is has already existed, but will not remain in the form in which we see it today.

Baha-ullah

A ll that exists in the world, without exception, is the seat of a movement of augmentation or of diminution. All that moves is alive, and the universal life is a necessary transformation: nothing is destroyed and nothing lost. If that is so, all is immortal, matter, life, intelligence, the breath, the soul, all that constitutes the living being.

Hermes

Nothing is born of nothing, nothing can be annihilated, each commencement of being is only a transformation.

Thales

Life and death, waking and sleep, youth and age are one and the same thing, for one changes into the other, that into this.

Heraclitus

All that is born, is corrupted to be born again.

Hermes

There is in all this only transformations of things one into another; there is no annihilation: a regulated order, a disposition of the ensemble, that is all. There is nothing else in a departure, it is only a slight change. There is nothing else in death, it is only a great change. The actual being changes, not into a non-existence, but into something it is not at present.

Epictetus

All manifest things are born from that which is unmanifest at the coming of the day, and when the night arrives they dissolve into the unmanifest; thus all this host of beings continually come into existence and they disappear at the advent of the night and are born with the approach of the day. But beyond the non-manifestation of things there is another and greater unmanifest state of being which is supreme and eternal, and when all existences perish, that does not perish.

Bhagavad Gita

The world possesses a thought and a sensation which is not like that of man nor so varied but superior and more simple. The world has only one sentiment, only one thought, to create all things and make them re-enter into itself.

Hermes

This universal order is the same for everything; neither God nor man has created it; it has always been, it is and will be always an eternally living Fire which kindles itself periodically and is again extinguished.

Heraclitus

The work of eternity is the world, which has not been produced once for all but is always produced by eternity. Thus it will never perish, for eternity is imperishable, and nothing is lost in the world because the world is enveloped in eternity.

Hermes

*
**

All goes, all returns, the wheel of existence turns forever. All dies, all reblossoms, the cycle of existence pursues its course forever. All is broken, and all again brought together, the same structure of existence is built and rebuilt forever. All separates and greets again, the ring of existence is faithful to itself forever. Existence is beginning at each moment.

Nietzsche

There where all ends, all is eternally beginning.

Hermes

Time which destroys the universe, must again create the worlds.

Mahabharata

Time takes away everything and gives everything; all changes but nothing is abolished, it is a thing immutable, eternal and always identical and one.

Giordano Bruno

There exists an unborn, an unproduced, uncreated, unformed. If this Permanent did not exist, there would be no possible issue for that which belongs to the world of the born, the produced, the created, the formed.

Udanavagga

But since there is a Permanent, there is also a possible issue for that which belongs to the world of the impermanence.

Udanavagga

The smallest drop of water united to the ocean no longer dries.

Hindu Saying

If the atom is lost in the sun of immensity, it

THE ETERNITY OF BEINGS   501

will participate, although a simple atom, in its eternal duration.

Farid-uddin Attar

*
*

What is it that is? It is that which was. And what is it that was? It is that which is. There is nothing new under the sun.

Giordano Bruno

The thing that hath been, it is that which shall be, and that which is done, it is that which shall be done: and there is no new thing under the sun. Is there anything whereof it may be said, See, this is new? It hath been already of old time which was before us.

Ecclesiastes

That which is not cannot come to being and that which is cannot cease to be.

Bhagavad Gita

That which is in all reality cannot begin to be nor be annihilated.

Schopenhauer

That which is was always and always will be.

Melissus

All that exists in the world, has always existed.

Antoine the Healer

There is no before or after: what will come tomorrow, is in fact in eternity.

Angelus Silesius

The question "What will happen" belongs to time; the soul is outside time. The soul has not been and will not be, it always is. If it were not, there would be nothing.

Tolstoy

Nothing is lost in the world because the world is enveloped in eternity.

Hermes

What is cannot perish.

Apollonius of Tyana

There is not a grain of dust, not an atom that can become nothing, yet man believes that death is the annihilation of his being.

Schopenhauer

Madmen are they, and counselled by an imprisoned mind and by narrow thoughts, who think that what was not before can be born or what is be utterly abolished in death and dissolution.

Empedocles

There is nothing, whether in its totality or its parts, which is not living:... how can that be corrupted which is a part of the incorruptible or something of God perish?

Hermes

The thought of God is the movement of the universe: never at any time can there perish a being, that is to say, a portion of God, for God contains all beings; nothing is outside him and he is outside of nothing.

Hermes

All beings are from all eternity.

Ashwaghosha

Thou Art

Birth and death are two limits; beyond those limits there is a sort of uniformity.

Tolstoy

And shall I then no longer be? Yes, thou shalt be, but thou shalt be something else of which the world will have need at that moment.

Epictetus

Can it be that change terrifies thee? But nothing is done without it.

Marcus Aurelius

Await with calm the moment of extinction or perhaps of displacement.

Marcus Aurelius

Restore to heaven and earth that which thou

owest unto them.... But of this dead man there is
a portion that is immortal.

Rig-veda

Thyself awaken thy self: then protected by
thyself and discovering thy own deepest secret,
thou shalt not change.

Hindu Saying

Thou remainest the same and thy years shall
not fail.

Hebrews

The moment that this mystery has been
unveiled to thy eyes that thou art no other than
Allah, thou shalt know that thou art thine own end
and aim and that thou hast never ceased and canst
never cease to be.

Mohyuddin ibn Arabi ·

If thou canst raise thy spirit above Space and

Time, thou shalt find thyself at every moment in eternity.

Angelus Silesius

Thou art.

Delphic Inscription

*
**

If in the morning you have heard the voice of celestial reason, in the evening you can die.

Confucius

Thence you can see that it is in a clear knowledge that is found our eternal life.

Ruysbroeck

Yea, though I walk through the valley of the shadow of death, I will fear no evil.

Psalms

I do not die, I go forth from Time.

Lebrun

I begin life over again after death even as the sun every day.

Book of the Dead

I was dead and, behold, I am alive forevermore.

Revelations

The day dies, I go towards repose, tomorrow evening the monastery bell shall ring out its accustomed voice, but no longer for me; I shall not hear it again as this I, but swallowed up in the great All I shall hear it still.

Anaximander

I have fought the good fight, I have finished my course, I have kept the faith. Henceforth there is laid up for me a crown of righteousness.

II Timothy

O death, where is thy sting? O grave, where is thy victory?... Death is swallowed up in victory.

I Corinthians

SECTION II

THE UNITY OF ALL

The Unity of Beings

To say eternal is to say universal.

Hermes

To represent constantly the world as one single being with one single soul and one single substance.

Marcus Aurelius

This world is a republic, all whose citizens are made of one and the same substance.

Epictetus

Thus even though it is not durable, there is no interruption in substance.

Lalita Vistara

Soul is one, Nature is one, life is one.

Hermes

In the multiple unity of the universal life, its innumerable species distinguished from one another by their differences are still united in such a way that the totality is one and all proceeds from oneness.

Hermes

The being of the universe is one and equally present in each individual, part or member of the universe, in such sort that the totality and each part make from the view-point of substance only one.

Giordano Bruno

All men are separated from each other by the body, but all are united by the same spiritual principle which gives life to everything.

Tolstoy

A river does not resemble a pond, a pond a tun, nor a tun a bucket: but in a pond, a river, a tun and a bucket there is the same water. And so too all men are different, but the spirit that lives in them all is the same.

Tolstoy

There is one body and one Spirit.

Ephesians

And all beings are resumed and reduced into one sole being, and they are one and all are He.

Zohar

All is Narayana, man or animal, the wise and the wicked, the whole world is Narayana, the Supreme Spirit.

Ramakrishna

The knowledge which sees one imperishable existence in all beings and the indivisible in things divided know to be the true knowledge.

Bhagavad Gita

The idea of thou and I is a fruit of the soul's ignorance.

Bhagavata Purana

Man understands his life only when he sees himself in each one of his kind.

Tolstoy

Let the sage unifying all his attentive regard see in the divine Spirit all things visible and invisible.

Manu

He who in his neighbour sees no other thing but God, lives with the light that flowers in the Divinity.

Angelus Silesius

He that thus knoweth, becometh the self of all beings. As is that Divinity, such is he. And as to that Divinity all beings have good will, even so to him that thus knoweth all beings have good will.

Brihadaranyaka Upanishad

That man who seeth the self in all beings and all beings in the self, has no disdain for anything that is.

Isha Upanishad

The sage regards the heart of every man in the millions of the crowd and sees only one heart.

Tseng Tse

*
**

When a corner of Maya, the illusion of individual life, is lifted before the eyes of a man in such sort that he no longer makes any egoistic difference between his own person and other men, that he takes as much interest in the sufferings of others as in his own and that he becomes suc-courable to the point of devotion, ready to sacrifice himself for the salvation of others, then that man is able to recognise himself in all beings, considers as his own the infinite sufferings of all that lives and must thus appropriate to himself the sorrow of the world. No distress is alien to him. All the torments which he sees and can so rarely soften, all the torments of which he hears, those even which it is

impossible for him to conceive, strike his spirit as if
he were himself the victim. Insensible to the
alternations of weal and woe which succeed each
other in his destiny, delivered from all egoism, he
penetrates the veils of the individual illusion: all
that lives, all that suffers is equally near to his
heart. He conceives the totality of things, their
essence, their eternal flux, the vain efforts, the
internal struggles and sufferings without end; he
sees to whatever side he turns his gaze man who
suffers, the animal who suffers and a world that is
eternally passing away. He unites himself henceforth to the sorrows of the world as closely as the
egoist to his own person. How can he having such
a knowledge of the world affirm by incessant
desires his will to live, attach himself more and
more to life and clutch it to him always more
closely? The man seduced by the illusion of individual life, a slave of his egoism, sees only the
things that touch him personally and draws from
them incessantly renewed motives to desire and to
will: on the contrary one who penetrates the
essence of things and dominates their totality,
elevates himself to a state of voluntary renunciation, resignation and true tranquillity.

Schopenhauer

Yes, from thenceforward, is there any suffering for one who sees this unity of the universe, this unity of life, this unity of the All? The separation between man and man, man and woman, man and child, nation and nation, that is the real cause of all the misery of the world. Now this separation is not at all real; it is only apparent, it is only on the surface. In the very heart of things is the unity which is forever. Go into yourself and you will find this unity between man and man, women and children, race and race, the great and the little, the rich and the poor, gods and men: all of us are one, even the animals, if you go down to a sufficient depth. And to the man who goes so far nothing can cause any illusion... where can there exist for him any illusion? What can deceive him? He knows the reality of everything, the secret of everything. Where can there exist any misery for him? What can he desire? He has discovered the reality of everything in the Lord who is the centre, the unity of all and who is the eternal felicity, the eternal knowledge, the eternal existence.

Vivekananda

*
**

If after having traversed the hall of wisdom, thou wouldst reach the valley of Beatitude, close, O disciple, thy senses to the great and cruel heresy of the separation which severs thee from the rest.

Book of Golden Precepts

One must learn to dissipate the shadow and live in the Eternal. And to that end thou shouldst live and breathe in all as all breathes in thee and feel that thou dwellest in all things in the self.

Book of Golden Precepts

Christianity says, "Love thy neighbour as thyself." And I say, "Recognise thyself in thy neighbour and that all men are in reality one and the same substance."

Schopenhauer

And let this be our thought, "Our bodies are different, but we have one and the same heart."

Mahavagga

Only after having the experience of suffering have I learned the kinship of human souls to each other.

Gogol

The Fundamental Equality of Beings

One can mount higher in a singular sort when the spirit soars above Time as high as eternity and there uniting itself with God becomes one thing with him and by that union knows and loves, not what is more or less noble, but all things in all things, considering them in that Object which is infinitely noble, all eminently reunited and in an equal degree of nobility. It is there that the spirit after it has raised itself above all that is, surpasses itself also and dwells imperturbable in an eternal repose, and the more it knows and loves, the more this eternity is affirmed and it becomes there itself eternal.

Tauler

The foundation of man's life is the dwelling in him of the divine Spirit equal in all men. And that is why men among themselves are all equal.

Tolstoy

The divine Spirit dwells in every man. How

can we make a difference among those who carry in themselves one and the same principle?

Tolstoy

Man is right when he believes that in all the world there is not a single being above him, but he errs when he thinks that there is on earth a single man beneath him.

Tolstoy

Only one who knows not that God lives in him can attribute to certain men more importance than to others.

Tolstoy

One could understand if men thought themselves unequal because one is stronger, loftier than another or more intelligent or more courageous or wiser or better. But it is not so that men are commonly distinguished from each other. It is deemed that men are not equal because one is called a count and the other a peasant, because one wears rich robes and the other wooden clogs.

Tolstoy

Nothing divides men so much as pride, whether it be the pride of the individual, of the family, of the class or of the nation.

Tolstoy

The proud man wishes to distinguish himself from others and deprives himself thus of the best joy of life, of a free and joyful communion with men.

Tolstoy

The vulgar say: "This is one of ours or a stranger." The noble regard the whole earth as their family.

Bhartrihari

Let the superior man regard all men who dwell within the four seas as his brothers.

Lun Yu

The man who recognises in his own soul the

supreme Soul present in all creatures, shows himself the same to all.

Manu

If there come into your assembly a man with a gold ring in goodly apparel and there come in also a poor man in vile raiment, and ye have respect to him that weareth the gay clothing and say unto him, "Sit thou here in a good place," and say to the poor man, "Stand thou there, or sit here under my footstool," are ye not then partial in yourselves and become judges of evil thoughts?

James

When I see the chaste women of respectable families, I see in them the Divine clothed in the robe of a chaste woman; and again, when I see the public women of the city seated on their verandahs in their raiment of immorality and shame, I see also in them the Divine at play after another fashion.

Ramakrishna

The Interdependence of Beings

All things are linked to each other and there is nothing that has not its relations. All beings are coordinate with each other and all contribute to the harmony of the world.

Marcus Aurelius

And all things depend one on the other and all are bound to each other,... all is that Ancient One and nothing is separate from him.

Zohar

All is coordinated in the universe. All things depend mutually on each other. All conspires to one sole end, not only in the individual whose parts are perfectly linked together, but anteriorly and to a higher degree in the universe.

Plotinus

What the members of the body are in the individual being, reasonable beings are in the same way even though separate, because they are formed to cooperate in one common work.

Marcus Aurelius

We all cooperate in one common work, some with knowledge and full intelligence, others without knowing it.

Marcus Aurelius

We are born to contribute to a mutual action like feet and hands. The hostility of men among themselves is against Nature.

Marcus Aurelius

Let us have always in our hearts this thought: I am a man and nothing that interests humanity is foreign to me. We have a common birth; our society resembles the stones of a road that sustain each other.

Seneca

One can be solitary in a secluded and

temporary environment; but each of our thoughts and each of our feelings finds, has found and will find an echo in humanity.

Amiel

No man liveth to himself.

St. Paul

*
**

We are every one members one of another.

Romans

All this universe, and in that word are comprised things divine and human, all is only one great body of which we are the members.

Seneca

This world is a people of friends, and these friends are first the gods and next men whom Nature has made for each other.

Epictetus

Listen to Nature: she cries out to us that we are all members of one family.

Saadi

All you have issued the one from the other.

Koran

Are we then so insensate as to forget that we are members one of the other?

St. Clement to the Corinthians

The members of the body which seem to be more feeble are necessary.

I Corinthians

And whether one member suffer, all the members suffer with it, or one member be honoured, all the members rejoice with it.

I Corinthians

The sons of Adam are the members of one

body, for in the creation they are made of one single nature. When fortune casts one member into suffering, there is no rest for the others. O thou who art without care for the pain of another, it is not fitting that one should give thee the name of man.

Saadi

See unceasingly the enchainment, the mutual solidarity of all things and all beings.

Marcus Aurelius

Even if thou wouldst, thou couldst not separate thy life from the life of humanity. Thou livest in humanity and by it and for it.

Marcus Aurelius

Thou art man, thou art a citizen of the world, thou art the son of God, thou art the brother of all men.

Marcus Aurelius

SECTION III

THE PRACTICE OF LOVE

The Law of Love

Love is the one truth.

Antoine the Healer

At all times love is the greatest thing.

Narada Sutra

An atom of love is to be preferred to all that exists between the two horizons.

Farid-uddin Attar

Love is the deliverance of the heart.

Anguttara Nikaya

All the means used in this life to acquire spiritual merit are not worth a sixteenth part of love, that deliverance of the heart: love unites and contains them all, and it illumines and shines out and radiates.

Itivuttaka

No radiance of the Spirit can dissipate the darkness of the soul below unless all egoistic thought has fled out of it.

Book of Golden Precepts

One should rely on love only, because it alone is the base of all strength and all regeneration.

Antoine the Healer

Love is immortal. Man obtaining it becomes perfect, becomes satisfied, becomes immortal. Once it is obtained, he desires nothing, is not afflicted, does not hate, is not diverted, strains no more after anything.

Narada Sutra

To love long, unweariedly, always makes the weak strong.

Michelet

Love is strong as death.

Song of Songs

*
**

It was by love that beings were created and it is commanded to them to live in love and harmony.

Baha-ullah

He that loveth another hath fulfilled the law.

Romans

Men are educated to consider wealth and glory above all things and they think only of getting as much as they can of glory and wealth. They ought to be educated to place love above all things and to consecrate all their powers to learn how to love.

Meh Ti

Each man, before he is Austrian, Serb, Turk or Chinese, is first of all a man, that is to say a thinking and loving being whose one mission is to fulfil his destiny during the short lapse of time that he is to live in this world. That mission is to love all men.

Tolstoy

The principal work of life is love. And one cannot love in the past or in the future: one can only love in the present, at this hour, at this minute.

Tolstoy

A sage was asked, "What is the most important work? who is the man the most important in life?" The sage replied, "The most important work is to love all men, because that is the life-work of each man. The most important man is the one with whom you have to do at this moment, because you can never know whether you will have to do with another."

Tolstoy

It is impossible to compel oneself to the love of others. One can only reject that which prevents love; and that which prevents is the love of one's material I.

Tolstoy

I know no other secret for loving except to love.

St. Francis de Sales

Let the disciple consecrate himself to love, not in order to seek for his own happiness, but let him take pleasure in love for the love of love.

Jataka Tales

To love, one must have no reservation, but be prepared to cast oneself into the flame and to give up into it a hundred worlds.... In this path there is no difference between good and evil; indeed with love neither good nor evil exists any longer.

Farid-uddin Attar

Reason cannot dwell with the madness of love: love has nothing to do with the human reason.

Farid-uddin Attar

But as we cannot love what is outside ourselves, we must love a being who is in us and who is not ourselves. Now it is only the universal Being who is such an one.

Pascal

It is not, in verity, yea, for the sake of the creature that the creature is dear to us, it is for the sake of the Self in all that the creature is dear. It is not, in verity, yea, for the sake of the all that the all is dear to us, it is for the sake of the One that the all is dear.

Brihadaranyaka Upanishad

My little children, let us not love in word, neither in tongue, but in deed and in truth. And hereby we know that we are of the truth.

I John

He that saith he is in the light and hateth his brother, is in the darkness even until now. He that loveth his brother abideth in the light and there is no occasion of stumbling in him. But he that hateth his brother is in darkness and walketh in darkness and knoweth not whither he goeth, because the darkness hath blinded his eyes.

I John

He that loveth not his brother abideth in death.

I John

We know that we have passed from death into life because we love our brothers.

I John

If a man say, I love God, and hateth his brother, he is a liar; for he that loveth not his brother whom he hath seen, how can he love God whom he hath not seen?

I John

No man hath seen God at any time. If we love one another, God dwelleth in us and his love is perfected in us.

I John

Let us say this clearly, my brothers, that we cannot reach unto God but by the intermediary of one who is like unto ourselves, by striving to love: God is not there where we think him to be, he is in ourselves. He dispenses love to us, he is love itself. Let us love then by him our neighbour.

Antoine the Healer

God is love, and he that dwelleth in love, dwelleth in God and God in him.

I John

He that loveth not, knoweth not God, for God is love.

I John

God is love and we are in our weakness imperfect gods.

Antoine the Healer

**

Beloved, let us love one another.

I John

For this is the message that ye have heard from the beginning, that we should love one another.

I John

The teaching of our master consists solely in this, to be upright in heart and to love one's neighbour as oneself.

Confucius

If ye fulfil the royal law, thou shalt love thy neighbour as thyself, ye do well; but if ye have respect to persons, ye commit sin.

James

Love one another.

John

This thing I command you that ye love one another.

John

Sustain one another in a mutual love.

Cullavaga

Owe no man anything but to love one another.

Romans

Love as brothers.

Peter

Be kindly affectioned one to another by brotherly love.

Romans

Let brotherly love continue.

Hebrews

Cherish in your hearts a love without any limit for the whole world and make your love to radiate over the world in all directions without any shadow of animosity or hate.

Metta Sutta

Whether you are standing or walking, whether you are seated or lying down, consecrate yourselves wholly to love: it is the best way of life.

Metta Sutta

Practise love and only love.

Narada Sutra

O my friends, plant only flowers of love in the garden of hearts.

Baha-ullah

To enter into the soul of each and allow each to enter into thine.

Marcus Aurelius

All beings aspire to happiness, therefore envelop all in thy love.

Mahabharata

If thou feel not love for men, busy thyself with thyself, handle things, do what thou wilt but leave men alone.

Tolstoy

Melt thy soul in the fire of love and thou wilt know that love is the alchemist of the soul.

Ahmed Halif

If thou lovest, God liveth in thee.

Tolstoy

Love thy neighbour and be faithful unto him.

Ecclesiasticus

Thou shalt love thy neighbour as thyself.

Leviticus

For all the law is fulfilled in one word, thou shalt love thy neighbour as thyself.

Galatians

Happiness Through Love

He who loves is in joy, he is free and nothing stops him.

Thomas à Kempis

Men will only be happy when they all love each other.

Tolstoy

Man cannot possess perfect happiness until all that separates him from others has been abolished in oneness.

Angelus Silesius

There can be no true freedom and happiness so long as men have not understood their oneness.

Channing

Man finds happiness only in serving his neighbour. And he finds it there because, rendering service to his neighbours, he is in communion with the divine spirit that lives in them.

Tolstoy

Why are we all joy when we have done a good action? Because each good action assures us that our true "I" is not limited to our own person, but exists in all that lives.

Tolstoy

When one lives for oneself, one lives only a portion of his true "I". When one lives for others, one feels his "I" expanding.

Tolstoy

The life of men is painful only because they do not know that the soul which is in each of us lives in all men. It is thence that comes animosity, that some are rich, others poor, some are masters, others workers, thence that come envy, hatred and all human torments.

Tolstoy

All the miseries of men are caused not by bad harvests, conflagrations, brigands, but simply because they live in discord. They are in discord because they do not believe in the voice of love who lives in them and calls them to union.

Tolstoy

One has no reason to regret when one dies, when one has lost money, property or house; all that does not belong to the man. One should have regret when man loses his real good, his greatest happiness: the faculty of loving.

Tolstoy

Be useful one to the other and the earth will flourish under your hands and wild animals will be obliged to respect your union.

Saadi

You will end by the discovery that the best means of health is to watch over the good health of others, and that the surest way to feel happy is to watch over the happiness of others.

Vivekananda

If man thinks only of himself and seeks everywhere his own profit, he cannot be happy. If thou wouldst really live for thyself, live for others.

Seneca

If thou livest for thyself alone, thou feelest thyself surrounded by enemies and the happiness of each an obstacle to thy own happiness. Live for others and thou wilt feel thyself surrounded by friends and the happiness of each will become thy happiness.

Tolstoy

When wilt thou understand that the true happiness is always in thy power and that it is the love for all men.

Marcus Aurelius

There is only one thing to do in order to be sure of being happy: it is to love the good and the wicked. Love always and thou wilt be happy always.

Tolstoy

Wilt thou that thy heart should be free from sorrow? Forget not the hearts that sorrow devours.

Saadi

Charity

Charity is the affection that impels us to sacrifice ourselves to humankind as if it were one being with us.

Confucius

He is truly great who has great charity.

Thomas à Kempis

And there is no more perfect life than that which is passed in the commerce and society of men when it is filled with charity towards one's neighbour.

Tauler

For charity covers a multitude of sins.

Peter

Let charity be without dissimulation.

Romans

Though I speak with the tongues of men and

of angels and have not charity, I am as a sounding brass or a tinkling cymbal. And though I have the gift of prophecy and understand all mysteries and all knowledge, and though I have all faith so that I could remove mountains, and have not charity, I am nothing. And though I bestow all my goods to feed the poor, and though I give my body to be burned, and have not charity, it profiteth me nothing. Charity suffereth long and is kind; charity envieth not, charity vaunteth not itself, is not puffed up, doth not behave itself unseemly, seeketh not her own, is not easily provoked, thinketh no evil, rejoiceth not in iniquity, but rejoiceth in the truth, beareth all things, believeth all things, hopeth all things, endureth all things. Charity never faileth.... And now abideth faith, hope, charity, these three: but the greatest of these is charity. Follow after charity.

I Corinthians

Walk in charity.

Ephesians

Let all your things be done with charity.

I Corinthians

Love All That Lives

The love for all that lives: all the religions teach it to us, the religion of the Brahmins, of the Buddhists, of the Hebrews, of the Chinese, of the Christians, of the Mohammedans. Therefore the most necessary thing in the world is to learn to love.

Tolstoy

Faith may vary with different men, in different epochs, but love is invariable in all.

Ibrahim of Cordova

What is virtue? It is sensibility towards all creatures.

Hitopadesha

Humanity does not embrace only the love of one's like: it extends over all creatures.

Chinese Proverb

The wise man acts towards all beings even as towards himself.

Mahabharata

To do no evil to any being, neither by action, nor by thought, nor by word; to will the good and to practise it: such is the eternal law of the good.

Mahabharata

He who does no evil to any is as if the father and mother of all beings.

Mahabharata

The superior man or the sage loves all beings that live, but has not for them the sentiments of humanity which he has for men. He has for men sentiments of humanity, but he does not love them with the love which he has for his father and mother. He loves his father and mother with filial love and he has for men sentiments of humanity. He has for men sentiments of humanity and he loves all beings that live.

Meng Tse

He must be good to animals, yet better to men.

Baha-ullah

The man to whom all men are strangers, who sees no other existence than his own and considers them like as phantoms capable only of serving his ends or of opposing them, sees the whole world extinguished at the moment of his death. On the contrary, he who recognises himself in others, even in all that lives, and pours his existence into that of every animated being, loses in dying only a feeble part of his life. Having destroyed the illusion which separated his consciousness from the rest of the world, he continues to live in all those whom he has loved.

Schopenhauer

*
**

Compassion toward animals is essentially bound up with goodness of character. Whoever is cruel to them cannot be good to men.

Schopenhauer

Hard to animals, hard to men.

Proverb

The poor animals who live in an obscure consciousness of dream possess many rights to love and compassion.

Jataka Tales.

One can recognise in those beings who are so far from us the principle of our own existence.

Schopenhauer

We feel in our conscience that that by which we live, that which we call our true "I" is the same not only in each man but also in a dog, a horse, a mouse, a fowl, a sparrow, a bee and even a plant.

Tolstoy

There is no beast on the earth, no bird flying on its wings that do not form a community like us.

Koran

When the incapacity to hurt and goodness are fully developed in him who has attained to the enlightened culture of the soul, there is a complete absence of enmity towards men, as also towards the animals who are near to him.

Patanjali

A man is not a master because he despotically subjects beings living at his mercy. He can be called a master who has compassion for all that lives.

Dhammapada

By not doing evil to creatures and mastering one's senses...one arrives here below at the supreme goal.

Laws of Manu

*
**

Discovering himself everywhere and in all things, the disciple embraces the entire world in a sentiment of peace, of compassion, of love large, profound and without limits, delivered from all wrath and all hatred.

Majjhima Nikaya

Without stick or sword, filled with sympathy and benevolence, let the disciple show to all beings love and compassion.

Majjhima Nikaya

Nourish in your heart a benevolence without limits for all that lives.

Metta Sutta

Thus thou shalt be in perfect accord with all that lives, thou shalt love men as thy brothers.

Book of Golden Precepts

Thou shalt not muzzle the ox that treads thy grain.

Deuteronomy

Be gentle, strike not an inoffensive animal, break not a domestic tree.

Pythagoras

All, even the vegetables, have rights to thy sensibility.

Chinese Proverb

Do no harm to an ant that is carrying its grain of corn, for it has a life, and sweet life is a good.

Firdausi

Have compassion, have pity for all beings that live. Let thy heart be benevolent and sympathetic towards all that lives.

Fo-shu-hing-tsan-king

Thou Shalt Not Kill

Thou shalt not kill.

Exodus

"Thou shalt not kill" relates not solely to the murder of man, but of all that lives.

Tolstoy

He that killeth an ox is as if he slew a man.

Isaiah

We are astonished to see that there have been and still are men who kill their kind in order to eat them. But the time will come when our grandchildren will be astonished that their grandparents should have killed every day millions of animals in order to eat them when one can have a sound and substantial nourishment by the use of the fruits of the earth.

Tolstoy

The man who consents to the death of an animal, he who kills it, he who cuts it up, the buyer, the seller, he who prepares the flesh, he who serves it and he who eats it, are all to be regarded as having taken part in the murder.

Laws of Manu

*
**

Whosoever seeketh to attain his personal happiness by maltreating or making to perish beings who were also striving after happiness... shall not find happiness.

Majjhima Nikaya

But the man who bringeth not by his own movement on living beings the pains of slavery and death and who desireth the good of all creatures, attaineth to happiness.

Laws of Manu

He who abstains from all violence towards beings, to the weak as to the strong, who kills not and makes not to kill, he, I say, is a Brahmin.

Dhammapada

Even as I are these, even as they am I, — identifying himself thus with others, the wise man neither kills nor is a cause of killing.

Sutta Nipata

What is dearest in the world to beings is their own self. Therefore from love for that own self which is so dear to beings, neither kill nor torment any.

Samyutta Nikaya

Shed not the blood of the beings that people the earth, men, domesticated animals, wild beasts and birds: out of the depths of thy soul rises a voice that forbids thee to shed blood, for the blood is the life, and thou canst not restore life.

Lamartine

Deliver them that are drawn unto death.

Proverbs

Thou shalt not kill.

Matthew

To Do No Hurt

The ills we inflict upon our neighbours follow us as our shadows follow our bodies.

Krishna

There is nowhere in this world, nor in the air, nor in the midst of the ocean any place where we can disembarrass ourselves of the evil we have done.

Dhammapada

The griefs thou puttest upon others shall not take long to fall back upon thyself.

Demophilus

Show kindness unto thy brothers and make them not to fall into suffering.

Chadana Sutta

None can reproach thee with injustice done?

It is too little. Banish injustice even from thy thought. It is not the actions alone, but the will that distinguishes the good from the wicked.

Democritus

The just man is not one who does hurt to none, but one who having the power to hurt represses the will.

Pythagoras

One must accustom oneself to say in the mind when one meets a man, "I will think of him only and not of myself."

Tolstoy

Whosoever thinketh with love, never offendeth any.

Antoine the Healer

If there be any other commandment, it is briefly comprehended in this saying. Thou shalt love thy neighbour as thyself. Love worketh no ill to his neighbour.

Romans

He is not a man of religion who does ill to another. He is not a disciple who causes suffering to another.

Dhammapada

Never to cause pain by thought, word or act to any living being is what is meant by innocence. Than this there is no higher virtue. There is no greater happiness than that of the man who has reached this attitude of good will towards all creation.

Vivekananda

Not to weary of well-doing is a great benediction.

Fo-shu-hing-tsan-king

Brothers, be good one unto another.

Baha-ullah

The charm of a man is in his kindness.

Proverbs

No Hatred

It is not pillage, assassinations and executions that are terrifying. What is pillage? It is the passing of property from some to others. That always has been and always will be and there is nothing in it that is terrifying. What are executions and assassinations? It is the passing of men from life to death. These passings have been, are and always will be, and there equally there is nothing that is terrifying. What is really terrifying is the hatred of men which engenders brigandage, theft and murder.

Tolstoy

But if the man who is animated by hatred, could by an effort of his hate enter even into the most detested of his adversaries and arrive in him to the very centre, then would he be greatly astonished, for he would discover there his own self.

Schopenhauer

Thou shalt not hate thy brother in thy heart.

Leviticus

Whosoever hateth his brother is a murderer: and ye know that no murderer hath eternal life abiding in him.

I John

There is no pollution like unto hatred.

Buddhist Text

Whosoever nourishes feelings of hatred against those who hate, will never purify himself, but one who in reply to hatred awakens love, appeases and softens those who are filled with hatred.

Dhammapada

That he may vanquish hate, let the disciple live with a soul delivered from all hate and show towards all beings love and compassion.

Majjhima Nikaya

F̲or it is an ancient and a true saying. Never shall hate be vanquished by hate, only by love is hatred extinguished.

Udanavagga

L̲et not one even whom the whole world curses, nourish against it any feeling of hatred.

Sutta Nipata

F̲or never in this world can hate be appeased by hate: hatred is vanquished only by love, — that is the eternal law.

Dhammapada

A̲h, let us live happy without hating those who hate us. In the midst of men who hate us, let us live without hatred.

Dhammapada

Nor Anger

He who is a friend of wisdom, must not be violent.

Fo-shu-hing-tsan-king

When we act with obstinacy, malice, anger, violence, to whom do we make ourselves near and like? To wild beasts.

Epictetus

Anger is an affection of the soul which, if it is not treated, degenerates into a malady of the body.

Apollonius of Tyana

It is by gentleness that one must conquer wrath, it is by good that one must conquer evil.

Dhammapada

One who returns not wrath to wrath, saves

himself as well as the other from a great peril: he is a physician to both.

Mahabharata

He that is slow to wrath is of great understanding.

Proverbs

But now put off all these, wrath, anger, malice, calumny, filthy communications out of your mouth.

Colossians

Let all bitterness and wrath and anger be put away from you.

Ephesians

Be ye angry, and sin not: let not the sun go down upon your wrath.

Ephesians

Let no evil communication proceed out of your mouth, but that which is good that it may minister grace unto the hearers.

Ephesians

He who makes to be heard words without harshness, true and instructive, by which he injures none, he, I say, is a Brahmin.

Dhammapada

I pledge myself from this day forward not to entertain any feeling of irritation, anger or ill humour and to allow to arise within me neither violence nor hate.

Buddhist Text

Not to Do unto Others

To repress anger will be possible to you if you show yourselves disposed towards those who commit faults as you would have them be to you if you had committed them yourselves.

Isocrates

To do to men what we would have them do to ourselves is what one may call the teaching of humanity.

Confucius

Nothing more allows of growth in humanity than to train oneself ardently in reciprocity, that is to say, to do to others as we would that they should do to us.

Meng Tse

The man who is sincere and careful to do nothing to others that he would not have done to him, is not far from the Law. What he does not desire to be done to him, let him not himself do to others.

Confucius

What we would not have done to us, we must not do to others.

Confucius

What we would not like being done to us, let us not do it to others.

Chung Yung

Let us act towards others as we would that they should act towards us: let us not cause any suffering.

Dhammapada

All things whatsoever ye would that men should do to you, do ye even so to them.

Matthew

What you wish others to do, do yourselves.

Ramakrishna

What you do not wish to be done to your-selves, do not do to other men.

Confucius

Do not do to others what you would not wish to suffer at their hands, and be to them what you would wish them to be to you.

Isocrates

What you love not in your superiors, do not to your inferiors; what you reprove in your infer-iors, do not to your superiors; what you hate in those who precede you, do not to those who follow you.... What you would not receive from those on your right, cast not upon those on your left.... Let this be the rule of your conduct.

Confucius

Do not thyself what displeases thee in others.

Thales

Do not to others what would displease thee done to thyself: this is the substance of the Law; all other law depends on one's good pleasure.

Mahabharata

I would act towards others with a heart pure and filled with love exactly as I would have them act towards me.

Lalita Vistara

With a heart pure and overflowing with love I desire to act towards others even as I would toward myself.

Buddhist Text

SECTION IV

THE SOLIDARITY OF ALL

Solidarity

Whatever is not of use to the swarm, is not of use to the bee.

Marcus Aurelius

The duty of man is to be useful to men: to a great number if he can, if not, to a small number, otherwise to his neighbours, otherwise to himself: in making himself useful to himself, he works for others. As the vicious man injures not only himself but also those to whom he might have been useful if he had been virtuous, likewise in labouring for oneself one labours also for others, since there is formed a man who can be of use to them.

Seneca

The most perfect man is the one who is most useful to others.

Koran

The just holds his own suffering for a gain

when it can increase the happiness of others.

Jataka Tales

If you act towards your like as a true brother, you do charity to yourselves.

Antoine the Healer

Look not every man on his own things, but every man also on the things of others.

Philippians

As every man hath received the gift, even so minister the same one to another.

I Peter

Aid each other in practising that which is good, but aid not each other in evil and injustice.

Koran

Let us help each other as friends that we may put a term to suffering.

Fo-shu-hing-tsan-king

Let us think that we are born for the common good.

Seneca

Let us be one even with those who do not wish to be one with us.

Bossuet

For all are called to cooperate in the great work of progress.

Antoine the Healer

*
**

Thou who hast been set in thy station of man to aid by all means the common interest...

Marcus Aurelius

Tire not being useful to thyself by being useful to others.

Marcus Aurelius

Think not that when the sins of thy gross form are overcome, thy duty is over to nature and to other men.

Book of Golden Precepts

There is no malady that can prevent the doing of thy duty. If thou canst not serve men by thy works, serve them by thy example of love and patience.

Tolstoy

Be not ashamed to be helped: thy end is to accomplish that which is incumbent on thee, like a soldier in the assault.

Marcus Aurelius

Never get done by others what thou canst thyself do.

Tolstoy

Recoil from the sun into the shadow that there may be more place for others.

Book of Golden Precepts

That it may be easy for thee to live with every man, think of what unites thee to him and not of what separates.

Tolstoy

As thou thyself art a complement of the organism of the city, let thy action likewise be a complement of the life of the city. If each of thy actions has not a relation direct or remote to the common end, it breaks the social life, it no longer allows it to be one, it is factious like the citizen who amid the people separates himself as much as it is in him from the common accord.

Marcus Aurelius

If thou hast seen an amputated hand or foot or a severed head lying separated from the rest of the body, even such he makes himself, as far as it is in him, who isolates himself from the All and acts against the common good.

Marcus Aurelius

What then is the duty of the citizen? Never

to consider his particular interest, never to calculate as if he were an isolated individual.

Epictetus

An offcast from the city is he who tears his soul away from the soul of reasoning beings, which is one.

Marcus Aurelius

A branch detached from the contiguous branch must needs be detached from the whole tree: even so a man separated even from a single man is detached from the whole society.

Marcus Aurelius

Have I done something for society? Then I have worked for myself, to my own advantage. Let this truth be present to thy mind and labour without ceasing.

Marcus Aurelius

We shall labour to our last sigh, we shall

never cease from contributing to the common good, serving every individual, helping even our enemies, exercising our talents and our industry. We know not an age destined to repose and, like the heroes of whom Virgil tells, our hair grows white under the helmet.

Seneca

Concord

The superior man lives in peace with all men without acting absolutely like them. The vulgar man acts absolutely like them without being in accord with them.

Confucius

An apostle of the truth should have no contest with any in the world.

Samyutta Nikaya

The beginning of strife is as when one letteth out water; therefore leave off contention before it be meddled with.

Proverbs

The disciple lives as a reconciler of those that are divided, uniting more closely those that are friends, establishing peace, preparing peace, rich in peace, pronouncing always words of peace.

Metta Sutta

What is there more precious than a sage? He sets peace between all men.

Shu Ching

But what a force is that of the sage who can live at peace with men without having the mobility of water and remain in the midst of them firm and incorruptible!

Confucius

*
**

Every kingdom divided against itself is brought to desolation and every city or house divided against itself shall not stand.

Matthew

Now I beseech you, brethren, that there be no divisions among you, but that ye be perfectly joined together in the same mind and in the same judgment.

I Corinthians

Have a care that ye sow not among men the seeds of discord.

Baha-ullah

Let us therefore follow after the things which make for peace and the things wherewith one may edify another.

Romans

Follow peace with all men.

Hebrews

Therefore if thou bring thy gift to the altar and there rememberest that thy brother hath aught against thee, leave there thy gift before the altar and go thy way, first be reconciled to thy brother and then come and offer thy gift.

Matthew

Respect

The sins that we do against men come because each one does not respect the Divine Spirit in his like.

Tolstoy

Respect man as a spiritual being in whom dwells the divine Spirit.

Tolstoy

Courtesy is the most precious of jewels. The beauty that is not perfected by courtesy is like a garden without a flower.

Buddhacharita

Let the superior man bear himself in the commerce of men with an always dignified deference, regarding all men that dwell in the world as his own brothers.

Confucius

Practising wisdom, men have respect one for another.

Lao Tse

Let us respect men, and not only men of worth, but the public in general.

Cicero

Show not respect in especial to those that are esteemed great and high in place, but treat with a like respect those that are judged to be small and at the bottom of the social ladder.

Tolstoy

Above all, respect thyself.

Pythagoras

If you observe in all your acts the respect of yourself and of others, then shall you not be despised of any.

Confucius

LIST OF AUTHORS AND SCRIPTURES

HINDU

Amritabindu Upanishad
Bhagavad Gita
Bhagavata Purana
Bhartrihari
Brihadaranyaka Upanishad
Chhandogya Upanishad
Harivansha
Hitopadesha
Isha Upanishad
Kaivalya Upanishad
Kapila
Katha Upanishad
Kena Upanishad
Laws of Manu
Mahabharata
Mundaka Upanishad
Narada Sutra
Panchatantra
Patanjali Prashna Upanishad
Prashnottaratrayamala
Raivatya Upanishad
Ramakrishna
Ramayana
Rig-veda
Sankhya Karika
Sankhya Pravachana
Sarvamedha Upanishad
Shankaracharya
Shatapatha Brahmana
Shwetashwatara Upanishad

Taittiriya Upanishad
Vemana
Vishnu Upanishad
Vivekananda

SIKH

Guru Granth Sahib

BUDDHIST

Abhidhammattha Sangaha
Amagandha Sutta
Anguttara Niyaka
Ashoka
Ashwaghosha
Book of Golden Precepts
Buddhacharita
Chadana Sutta
Chinese Buddhist Texts
Cullavaga
Dhammapada
Digha Niyaka
Fa-ken-pi-u
Fo-shu-hing-tsan-king
Itivuttaka
Jataka Tales
Japanese Buddhist Texts
Lalita Vistara
Lotus Sutra
Mahamangala Sutta

Mahaparinibbana Sutta
Mahavagga
Mahayana Buddhist Formula
   of Devotion
Majjhima Niyaka
Metta Sutta
Nidhikama Sutta
Padhama Sutta
Pali Canon
Sangita Sutta
Samyutta Niyaka
Sonadanda Sutta
Sutra in Forty-two Articles
Sutta Nipata
Udanavagga
Uttama Sutta
Vinaya Pitaka

Shih Ching
Shu Ching
Tsang Yung
Tseng Tse
Tsu Tse

JAPANESE

Kobo Daishi
Mikado Shujaku
Minamoto Sanetomo
Ryonin
Sojo Henjo
Takedo Shingen
Tyotomi Hideyoshi
Zeisho Aishako
Zesho Atsuko

CHINESE

Chin Ku Li
Confucius
Chuang Tse
Chung Yung
Huai-nan Tse
I Ching
Kin-yuan-li-sao
Kun Yu
Lao Tse
Li Chi
Lun Yu
Meh Ti
Meng Tse

EGYPTIAN

Egyptian Book of the Dead
Egyptian Funeral Rites
Hymn to Ptah
Ptah-hotep

MEXICAN

Totaku-ko-Nozagual

ZOROASTRIAN

Minokhired
Zend-Avesta

GREEK

Classical

Anaxagoras
Anaximander
Aristotle
Bias of Priene
Chilon
Delphic Inscriptions
Democritus
Demophilus
Diogenes of Apollonia
Empedocles
Epictetus
Euripides
Heraclitus
Homer
Isocrates
Melissus
Menedemus
Orphic Hymns
Philolaus
Phocylides
Plato
Proclus
Pythagoras
Socrates
Solon
Sophocles
Thales
Theognis

Post-Classical

Apollonius of Tyana

Epictetus
Hermes Trismegistus
Iamblichus
Plotinus
Plutarch
Porphory

ROMAN

Cato
Cicero
Horace
Macrobius
Marcus Aurelius
Philo Judaeus
Sallust
Senoca

JUDAIC

The Old Testament

Deuteronomy
Ecclesiastes
Exodus
Ezekiel
Genesis
Hebrews
Hosea
Isaiah
Jeremiah
Job
Joshua

Judges
Leviticus
Proverbs
Psalms
Song of Songs
Zechariah

Apocrypha

Book of Wisdom
Ecclesiasticus
Esdras

Other

Abraham ibn Ezra
Kabbalah
Maimonides
Talmud
Zohar

CHRISTIAN

The New Testament

The Four Gospels:
Luke, Saint
John, Saint
Mark, Saint
Matthew, Saint
The Epistles:
James, Saint
John, Saint
Paul, Saint: To the
   Corinthians; Colossians;
   Galatians; Ephesians;

Thessalonians; Timothy;
   Titus; Phillipians
Peter, Saint
Revelation of Saint John

Other

Angelus Silesius
Augustine, Saint
Barnabas, Saint
Basil, Saint
Bossuet, Jacques Bénigne
Catacombs Inscriptions
Clement, of Alexandria, Saint
Clement, of Corinth, Saint
Cyprian, Saint
Eckhart, Meister
Epistles to Diognetus
Fénelon, François de
Francis de Sales, Saint
Luther, Martin
Polycarp, Saint
Ruysbroeck, Jan Van
Salignac de la Mothe
Shepherd of Hermes
Tauler, Johannes
Thomas à Kempis

ISLAMIC

Ahmed Halif
Jalal-uddin Rumi
Farid-uddin Attar
Firdausi

Gulshen-i-Raz
Ibn Mazud
Ibrahim of Cordova
Mahmud Hasiha
Mohammed
Mohyuddin ibn Arabi
Omar Khayyam
Rose of Bakanali, The
Saadi

BABISM AND BAHAISM

Bab, The
Baha-ullah

MODERN WESTERN
    AUTHORS

Amiel, Henri Frederic
Antoine the Healer
Bacon, Francis
Boehme, Jacob
Bruno, Giordano
Carlyle, Thomas
Catinat, Nicolas
Channing, William Ellery
Emerson, Ralph Waldo
Franklin, Benjamin
Goethe, Johann Wolfgang
    Von

Gogol, Nikolai Vasilyevich
Hugo, Victor
Huxley, Aldous
Kant, Immanuel
Lacordaire, Jean Baptiste
    Henri
Lebrun, Charles
Leibnitz, Gottfried Wilhelm
Lichtenberg, Georg
    Christoph
Michelet, Jules
Montaigne, Michel Eyquem
Nietzsche, Friedrich Wilhelm
Novalis
Oersted, Hans Christain
Pascal, Blaise
Pasteur, Louis
Petrarch, Francesco
Pico della Mirandola
Rousseau, Jean Jacques
Ruskin, John
Schopenhauerr, Arthur
Spinoza, Benedict Baruch
Thoreau, Henry David
Tolstoy, Leo Nikolayovich
Vauvenargues, Luc de
    Clapiers
Voltaire, François Maire
    Arouet de
William the Silent